Max Rafferty on

EDUCATION

Max Rafferty on EDUCATION

by Max Rafferty

The Devin-Adair Company
New York 1968

Contents

CONTENTS

Education's
Twelve Labors

in which the nature of the headache is duly diagnosed

Our Awakening Giant

A giant stirs in the land today.

He tosses his head restively. He moves hesitantly as yet, but the rumbling of his awakening is beginning to shake the nation. His hands wield the thunderbolts which alike can blast or forge the future.

His name is "Education in Depth" and he waits upon our commands.

Long ago, a poetic people half the world away personified the power and the undaunted will of Man in the form of a demigod, massive and mighty, created to serve humanity. They called him Hercules and gave him twelve great labors to perform. In due time they were accomplished, and a Golden Age came upon the ancient world and shone for a season with such a shimmer and dazzle of radiance that still today, after two millenia and more, we look back with an ache in our hearts and a wistful turning of our heads to those magic days when men lived and built and thought like gods.

The Golden Age of Greece will not return, but we educators have it in our means to build a new and finer one in our own era, one attuned to the temper of our times and to the century of science in which we live. But first we too have certain labors to perform.

In the pages ahead we shall look at the new Twelve Labors with which our own awakening giant must wrestle.

THE FIRST LABOR
An End to 'Life Adjustment' Education

Ever hear these catch-phrases mouthed around your local school?

"Facts are the least important things we teach the children. They forget all of them within a short time, anyhow."

and

"Memorization is stultifying. Besides, how do we know these names and places and events are important enough to memorize? Is anything, really?"

and

"Johnny isn't adjusting to his peer group properly. Sometimes I don't think he's interested in what they're doing. If this keeps on, Johnny may even grow up *unpopular!*"

All these and many more like them are the watch-words and the war-cries of Progressive Education. The exponents of this philosophy hold the only eternal verity to be that of constant change and flux. All values are relative to them. All truths are mutable. All standards are variable. So the only thing worth teaching youngsters is to adjust to their environment, to practice endless "togetherness" and "democratic socializing," to be easily and comfortably and happily accepted by their "peer group."

But despite what these spreaders of the gospel according

to St. John Dewey have been drip-dripping into your ears and minds for 30 years and more, I say to you that the purpose of a school is not to make pupils popular or well-adjusted or universally approved.

It is to make them *learned*.

It is to teach them to use the intellectual tools which the race, over the centuries, has found to be indispensable in the pursuit of truth.

If the men and women who preceded us on this continent and who conquered it and who made it safe for us to live on had adopted the philosophy of "adjustment to environment" as their supreme goal in life, we their descendants would be living still along a narrow strip of the Atlantic seaboard in log cabins, and fighting off Indians. For this would have represented optimum "adjustment" to the environment which they found.

Instead, our fathers preferred to adjust their environment to themselves, or rather to that which they hoped someday to become. And in so doing they built for us a nation which is at once the wonder and the envy of the human race.

Do those who run your schools believe that "life adjustment" should be the main goal of instruction? If they do, this is Progressive Education.

Do they teach things like "social studies" and "social living" and "language arts" instead of history and geography and civics and English?

Do your school people tell you that report cards are old-fashioned? Do they teach reading predominantly through the "look-say," Egyptian-hieroglyphic method instead of through the phonics method?

All these things are the brand and trademark of Progressive Education. And Progressive Education, regardless of what your educational apologists are currently calling it, is bad education.

I tell you that the schools exist to teach organized, disciplined, systematic subject matter to the children. I tell you further that the schools are the only societal agencies specifically charged with the performance of this vital function. And I say finally that if the schools do not so teach subject matter, the children are never going to learn it.

"Life adjustment" is taught by the home, by the church, by society itself in a hundred ways. Only the school can forge for the child the wonderful, shining, sharp-edged sword of subject matter.

This is the new philosophy, Education in Depth. It holds that in this life, this world, this universe, there is such a thing as Truth, and that education consists in seeking out that truth, no matter where it may be nor how deeply it may lie hidden. Mortal man may never hold it in his hands, true enough, but the very quest cannot but ennoble those who take part in it.

Which do you want for your children? The pablum of in-groupness or the strong meat of subject matter? Geography as the study of land and water formations, or geography as "Tom and Susan's Airplane Trip to Niagara Falls"? English as grammar and punctuation and literature, or English as "How to Talk on the Telephone" or "How to Become a Successful Toastmaster"?

As an educator, I have devoted my life to a struggle against this thing called Progressive Education which has

ruined so many lives and which has done its best to produce a generation of quasi-illiterates.

But so long as the schools are yours, the final choice is
yours also.

See you to it.

THE SECOND LABOR
The Fight for Local Control

Up until a few years ago, nobody seemed to care very
much who ran America's schools. Local school boards
attracted relatively few citizens to their meetings and even
fewer to their elections. In education as in a lot of other
things, we seemed content to let George do it.

And then along came Sputnik and things all of a sudden
became quite, quite different. As soon as massive state and
federal financial aid began to be pumped into the surprised
veins of local school districts, it was almost funny to watch
the politicians sit up and take notice.

Chicago recently found out in several ways how hard
it is for even great cities to maintain the independence of
their own schools when the vast Washington bureaucracies
begin to pour in money and to throw their weight around.

You see, there are always strings attached to the shiny
packages of federal goodies.

First, there was the weird "test" which Uncle Sugar
dreamed up as an accompaniment to his largesse. It asked
some rather prying, highly personal questions of the small
fry, designed apparently to see whether the kids were de-
veloping "proper" attitudes toward Mom and Pop, each

other and life in general. What constitutes a "proper" viewpoint is, of course, to be decided by the bureaucrats of the Department of Health, Education and Welfare.

When the Chicago school authorities quite properly balked at this kind of Orwellian brain tampering, Washington pouted, sulked and eventually used an acute racial housing problem as an excuse to brandish a $30 million thunderbolt forged of federal aid money under the new legislation. It took Daley, Dirksen and darned near the Deity to pry Chicago's money out of the hands of the power-hungry officials in the national capital.

This is a classic illustration of why our ancestors reserved certain key powers, including education, to the states, and denied them to the federal government.

One thing they didn't count on, of course, was the evolution of a Supreme Court which would interpret the Constitution not according to how it was written but according to how the learned justices thought it *should* have been written. As a result, we have Washington barging into local school districts all across the country and the end is hard even to imagine.

When Lord Acton said, "All power corrupts, and absolute power corrupts absolutely," he wasn't kidding, as we are now beginning to see.

A couple of generations ago, a stunt like this one would have brought our grandfathers out into the streets ready to fight. Why? Because they would have recognized arbitrary federal interference with the right of local individuals to govern themselves and to determine the educational destinies of their own children as a long, long step toward tyranny. It always has been.

Children do not belong to the state. They do not belong to us educators, either. They belong to their parents and to nobody else. And don't you forget it.

Because if you *do* forget it and let the kids become wards of an all-powerful government, you won't have to look forward with fear and trembling any more to that dread year 1984. It will be here, considerably ahead of schedule.

Nobody ever said that local control of our own affairs was more economical than statism, or more efficient, or more honest, for that matter. It isn't. It's just freer, that's all. That's all it has ever been. It has always been expensive to establish it and to keep it going—expensive in terms of money and sometimes in terms of human lives. But to the men who fought the King, the Redcoats, the Hessians, the Indians, and who would have fought the Devil himself two hundred years ago to gain freedom for their children, local self-government was worth whatever it cost, paid in whatever coin was necessary at the time.

So sit back with your six-packs and your backyard barbecues every time there's a school board election. Skip voting. After all, what good is your one lonely little vote? It's so much more convenient just to let Washington handle these details, isn't it? Abdicate your right to determine what Junior's schooling is going to be like. Turn Junior over to the U.S. Commissioner.

Of course, this is the way empires are lost, and independence, and individual liberty. But what of it? These things are so inconvenient, after all . . .

THE THIRD LABOR
Keeping Education a Profession

Once upon a time, the precious coinage of our common language was pure and unalloyed. Words meant what they said and with no nonsense about them. Among them were the two little adjectives "legal" and "proper." No one even thought of confusing them.

It's always been legal, for instance, for a minister's wife to work as a strip-teaser at the local burlesque house. But it wasn't proper, so she didn't.

Similarly, a bearded beatnik who regards his country with contempt enjoys the legal right to offer himself for enlistment in the Marine Corps, but it would be neither proper nor intelligent for him to do so.

Recently, however, there has been a lot of talk throughout my profession of education about the right of school teachers to engage in strikes, boycotts and collective bargaining in order to get higher pay and better working conditions, and those two small but important words "legal" and "proper" seem to be getting all fouled up.

No one is arguing about the right of organized labor to use the weapons of labor. There is quite a bit of arguing, however, as to the propriety of a learned profession's using these weapons.

We schoolmen have paid lip service all our lives to the ideal of professionalization. We have clamored down the years for equal recognition with medicine and the law and the ministry. We have talked unendingly about the need for "professional salaries." Some of us have even gone so far as to chide laymen for meddling in educational matters by tut-tutting:

"Oh, come now! You wouldn't try to tell the head surgeon at the Mayo Clinic how to perform an operation, would you?"

Yet today an awful lot of my professional colleagues seem just about ready to chuck the whole idea of education as a learned profession in favor of unionized skilled labor.

From New York to Utah, we see the sorry spectacle of teachers proclaiming their "right" to strike and demonstrating it by leaving their classrooms unsupervised and their pupils uninstructed.

We seem obsessed with the need to impress the public with our "power"—a strange word in the mouths of educators—and to develop punitive weapons like "sanctions" for use against local school boards which may dare to disagree with us as we thunder and threaten from Mount Sinai.

Well, I may be badly misinformed but I don't recall any instances where the Mayo Clinic surgical staff went out on strike because the management was unwilling to raise fee rates. Neither do I remember many examples of attorneys picketing their law firms because they didn't approve of the legal philosophy of the senior partner.

Who suffers when we educators do anything which interferes with the instructional program in a school district? Not the board members. Not the voters. Not even the parents. They've already had their education.

No, it's always the children who suffer—the very ones we are sworn to help, not hurt. How can we expect anyone to take seriously our protestations that we are indeed a profession, deserving "professional" salaries, when we insist on using such unprofessional tactics in order to achieve our objectives?

To each his own. To labor, the proper and legal weapons of labor. To a profession, the proper and legitimate weapons of a profession: logic, reasoning and persuasion.

After all, if we teachers can't educate the public into doing the things it ought to do, maybe we are in the wrong business. We certainly should be able to talk people into doing what is right without having to pummel them into it. If we can't, who on earth can?

We educators work for the people. They don't work for us. As specialized experts, we deserve decent treatment. If we don't get it, we can do what other professionals do: go somewhere else and work.

We can also exercise our Constitutional right to petition and to remonstrate and to use the ballot to change policies in the school districts in which we live and work.

But we have no right under the sun to threaten and to bully and to coerce.

These things may perhaps be legal but they can never be proper. Not for us. At least we can keep our semantics straight.

THE FOURTH LABOR
The Need for Better Books

The most glaring, technicolored example of what a generation of Progressive Education has done to our schools is to be found in the elementary textbooks.

Over the last 30 years, our major publishing houses have been worked over by two formidable conditioners: (1) the behavioristic psychologists, who insisted on the children's being conditioned to cooperate at any cost and with everybody, and (2) the curriculum experts and reading supervisors, who ruled out of the books anything more interesting than *The Visit to the Dairy* and anybody more exciting than Dick and Jane.

The result has been what journalist Jenkin Lloyd Jones once dubbed the kids' books in a felicitous phrase: "sawdust sandwiches."

In case you haven't been browsing through your children's textbooks recently, here are a few things which are more than slightly wrong with them:

(1) *Vocabulary.* It mainly isn't, you know, like the little man upon the stair. We found out recently that we expose our first graders to about one-third as many "new" words as the Russians give their beginners. And the words we do give them are usually spoonfed in a horridly repetitive, dreadfully boring "story" guaranteed to hamstring in advance any latent interest in reading which the poor youngsters may have possessed.

"See me jump," said Billy.

"See me jump," said Betty.

"I can jump," said Billy.

"I can jump," said Betty.

A pox upon such doggerel! Surely nobody, not even a moron, would have the slightest itch to turn Page 1 in order to find out if Billy and Betty were still jumping on Page 2.

And consider the poor primary instructor faced with

printed fatuity year after year. It brings to mind the story —perhaps apocryphal—of the first-grade teacher who saved enough of her salary to purchase a tiny compact car, only to have a truck back over it and squash it into rubble the first night she parked it in front of her apartment. Running out on the porch and wringing her hands, she lamented in the only language she knew: "Oh, oh, oh. Look, look look. Damn, damn, damn."

(2) *Interest.* Once again, the "readers" are the worst offenders. They are full of stories by people who, to put it as charitably as possible, are not exactly in the same class as Charles Dickens or Sir Walter Scott. Oh, let's be blunt about it. They are people no one ever heard of. They write dreadful little stories with such titles as *How Billy Helped His Team* and *A Brand New Job for a Tractor* in which the characters are one-dimensional, the plots are imbecilic and the climaxes are nonexistent.

(3) *Importance of Content.* The so-called "social studies" books in the grades are the biggest culprits. If they teach the kids any history, it is purely accidental. In California we had until recently a fifth grade text which devoted page after jaded page to such trivia as how the pioneer women made linsey-woolsey clothing for their children and how their husbands pulled stumps out of corn fields with the aid of ox teams, while completely failing even to mention such events as the Monroe Doctrine and such men as Daniel Webster.

When you look through Junior's school books, you might try to find the great children's classics. Don't hold your breath. Echoes of Meg, Beth and Amy, the Tin

Woodman and the Frog Footman have faded from the books and so from the experience of the children.

Friendship with David Balfour and Captain Nemo, Jim Hawkins and Little Alice used to be part and parcel of the literary birthright of every American child. Not any more.

If you were to ask the child "experts" and the reading consultants why we can't give the youngsters the glory of *Treasure Island* and the wonder of *The Three Musketeers* any more, they will look at you pityingly and tell you that such classics are far too "mature" for today's children.

And if they are too mature indeed, whose fault is it?

They were not too mature for the children who grew up to be our grandparents. Are the kids of today more stupid than the kids of 50 years ago? I don't believe it.

Can it be that by giving pap to the kids we've accustomed them to pap? Could it also be that by giving them a little good, solid, literary meat we might even get them to like it?

I say "yes." Many publishers are even now preparing better, more rewarding, more interesting books for our children. For Pete's sake, let's encourage them.

And remember: if you want this type of fine new reading material to replace what your school is now offering under the guise of textbooks, you will probably have to fight for it. So get with it. For the kids' sake.

THE FIFTH LABOR
How to Get Top Teachers

We have lots of good teachers in our schools. We need lots more. It's hard to get them because:

(1) Universal compulsory education has compelled us to recruit as teachers persons who formerly would have been plumbers, ribbon clerks and insurance salesmen.

(2) Industry's cut-throat competition for specially qualified personnel has raided thousands of classrooms of our best teachers.

(3) Stupid, inane course requirements for the teaching credential have nauseated an awful lot of fine potential teachers to the point where they have said "To heck with it!" and have gone into something else.

Mass education has profoundly affected teaching as a profession. Prior to this century there had always been enough teachers to go around. Every generation had produced its normal quota of "born" teachers—dedicated individuals who simply had to teach, much as Chopin had to write music and Michelangelo had to carve statues. There never were too many of these people, you understand, but inasmuch as not everyone went to school, there were enough teachers to get by.

Universal education upset the age-old balance between pupil and teacher permanently and drastically. Suddenly we had to draft people into the profession who in the old days would never have thought of becoming teachers. The more teachers which is still with us, and which threatened torrent of children brought with it a built-in demand for

for quite a while to water down irrevocably all standards of teacher training and selectivity.

Then, in connection with the piratical activities of industry, there is the question of seed corn.

Even the poorest sharecropper knows that when he's so broke and hungry and desperate that he starts eating the seed corn he was saving for next year's planting, he's in mighty bad shape.

Seed corn is not confined to farming.

For almost 20 years now both industry and science have been living on their seed corn, in the persons of untold thousands of superior teachers who have been extracted from our local school systems with forceps made of thousand-dollar bills. Since 1945, I have seen my best teachers, especially in science and math, quit their chosen careers, reluctantly but inevitably, to take jobs paying four times as much in private industry.

Every one of them in the course of a long life of teaching would have influenced thousands of young people and undoubtedly would have steered many of them into scientific and industrial specialties. What kind of shortsighted folly is it for the big brains who do the hiring for our vast scientific and industrial organizations to blithely cut their own throats in this way? Why do they solve temporary problems for themselves at the cost of king-size headaches for their successors in the 1980s?

What they ought to be doing, of course, is working to get teachers' salaries up at least enough so that they won't have to neglect and handicap their own children while they are instructing other people's children. And while they are doing this, they ought to declare a moratorium on luring professional educators away from their vital place in our countless classrooms.

Finally, there is the absolutely essential need to cut out the guff and the trivia in our teacher training programs. There is still far too much nonsense, far too many courses in "Principles of Education," followed by "Principles of Elementary Education" and in due time "Principles of Secondary Education" and so on, ad infinitum and sometimes ad nauseam.

Bright-eyed, eager-beaverish would-be teachers are still having their enthusiasm cooled and their ardor chilled by dull, dreary, teachers-college emphasis on such nonintellectual goals as "life adjustment," "togetherness" and "ingroupness," when what they want to study is subject matter, preferably in their own chosen fields.

My own state of California recently threw out the old standards for teacher training, cut the so-called "methodology" courses in half and took the whole thing out of the hands of the "education" professors in favor of putting it under the control of the entire liberal arts faculty.

We think this is going to work a revolution in attracting able, idealistic recruits into our teaching ranks. A certain glamor, a certain prestige will attach to the trained subject-matter expert in the classroom which unfortunately does not apply to the practitioners of "peer-group acceptance" and "environmental adjustment."

California's revolution, incidentally, is eminently exportable.

I recommend it to you.

THE SIXTH LABOR
A New Philosophy of Teacher Training

Who is the last defender of Progressive Education?

Who refuses to recognize the fact that the great American public wants its public schools to teach Education in Depth?

Who insists upon indoctrinating generation after generation of young teachers with the dogmas of John Dewey?

I'll tell you who: the teachers colleges.

With a few honorable exceptions, the Maginot Line of the old, discredited "life adjustment" philosophy sometimes known as Progressive Education is currently the teacher training institutions and the schools of education in our colleges and universities.

Everyone with eyes to see knows that Progressive Education under its many masks and innumerable aliases is today very much on the defensive and fighting delaying actions all across the land. Yet far too many professors of education are still hanging on grimly and stubbornly to the Dewey-eyed doctrines of the Thirties and the Forties.

They are still telling young, would-be teachers about the evil effects of homework, the danger lurking in exposing first-graders to the alphabet and the need to abolish subject-matter, A-B-C-D-F report cards because they serve as mere status symbols for the parents and encourage "competition" (dreadful word!) for grades among the pupils.

They sneer at learning for the sake of learning.

They discourage and give low grades to any of their student teachers who insist upon the organized, disciplined, systematic presentation of subject matter as their principal interest and function.

In countless professional journals, they carry on a vicious and vindictive guerrilla warfare against any and all educational reformers who show any inclination to upset the cozy, comfortable kingdom which these professors of education have built for themselves at the expense of both basic education and the taxpayer's pocketbook.

Like Paul on the road to Damascus, the education professors feel that Divine Certainty has been unveiled to them and that anybody who dares to question their own exclusive version of Revelation is not only both foolish and mulish, but also more than a little wicked.

For the past two decades and more, like the Bourbons of old they have learned nothing and forgotten nothing.

Public school systems can have their philosophies and policies changed for them by the people via the ballot box.

But teacher training institutions are far less responsive to the demands of public opinion. Most of them are controlled by boards of regents or trustees who are under no obligation to meet the needs and wishes of the citizenry because they are not selected or reappointed by the citizenry.

The results we see all around us: too many of our teacher-training institutions are so badly out of step with the great parade of public opinion that they run the very grave and real risk of finding themselves on another street entirely from the rest of the marchers.

Clearly, something is going to have to give. This kind of entrenched, arrogant opposition to the new philosophy called Education in Depth is reminiscent of nothing so much as the old Chinese mandarin hierarchy which dominated the Celestial Empire for so many hundreds of years and which effectively prevented any sort of change or reform until the "foreign devils" finally poured over the Great Wall and into the port cities to overthrow the dynasty.

The colleges are going to have to scrap their outmoded insistence upon the "how" of teaching to the virtual exclusion of the "what."

We can no longer afford to educate our teachers along the Progressive Education lines characteristic of a bygone era as out of date as high-button shoes and "23 Skiddoo!" and then turn them out of our teachers colleges to try to make a living in local school districts which are supported and populated by people who are fervent converts to the new Education in Depth.

The places where teachers are taught to teach must now accept the overwhelming verdict of the people and couch their training programs in terms of Education in Depth as they currently couch them in terms of "life adjustment."

Of course teachers have to have methodology courses. Of course they have to learn the "how" as well as the "what" of teaching. But for years now subject matter has been scanted and stinted in favor of methodology insofar as teacher trainees have been concerned.

In my own state, I am presently pushing for exams in basic subjects like math and English to be administered as a prerequisite for the granting of the first teaching credential. Law and medicine do this. I can see no reason why education shouldn't.

The big roadblock is the attitude of the teacher-training institutions. It is apparently going to be necessary to drag them kicking and screaming into the seventh decade of the twentieth century.

THE SEVENTH LABOR
The Need to Reward Superior Teaching

Talking about merit pay for teachers is the best way I know to start a fight in my profession. An educator who comes out flat-footedly for merit pay is about as popular these days as Stokely Carmichael at an American Legion convention.

Just the same, in any discussion of the problems of modern education, this one simply has to be dealt with.

There will be no permanent improvement in the caliber and quality of teaching in these United States until we educators stop thinking of ourselves as so unique and special that the ordinary processes of evaluation and promotion do not apply to us.

There is no point in beating around the bush or in trying to disguise what we're really talking about.

The only way to make teaching attractive enough to compete on any kind of equal basis with science and industry for the services of superior people is to acknowledge that some teachers are better than others and pay them accordingly. Otherwise, our best talent will continue to be subject to raids by other occupations which can offer such incentive pay for superior work.

Private industry has always followed a policy of giving better pay and faster promotion to employees who did their work better than other employees. Nobody seems unduly concerned over the fact that someone has to make the decision as to what that little word "better" really means. Nobody seems too worried, either, over the problem presented by a "subjective" rating depending heavily upon somebody's opinion.

After all, what other kind of a rating is there?

No, industry and business just go blissfully on raising the pay of their better employees despite the theoretical disadvantages of individual injustice and decline of employee morale. In much the same way, I suppose, the bumblebee flies happily from flower to flower, not knowing that his winged activity was proved a long time ago to be aerodynamically impossible.

My own profession, however, through its great organizations and hierarchies, has long and bitterly opposed merit pay, and still does, ostensibly for the ridiculous reason that no objective device for measuring "merit" as yet exists.

The reason I call this argument ridiculous is that when I was studying to be a teacher more than a quarter of a century ago the identical argument was used to justify opposition to merit pay. Surely if the profession had been serious it would long ago have developed some sort of acceptable instrument.

In reality merit pay has been opposed for another reason entirely: because a lot of us professional educators have inferiority complexes and believe that it is somehow "undemocratic" to pay certain teachers more than others merely because they are better teachers.

What we are really saying is that we shrink from comparison, that rather than see somebody else rewarded financially for his ability while we perhaps might be passed over, we are going to oppose the whole principle of more pay for better work.

We come up with a whole pack of rationalizations to excuse this attitude. We profess to be scared that an evil school administrator will use merit pay as a weapon to terrorize his demoralized faculty or that a venal school board will seize upon merit pay as a means to keep over-all salaries in the sweatshop category. But this is mere window dressing. Every workable merit pay plan I've ever known has recognized these obvious dangers and taken them into account.

How do teachers get raises now? Why, on the basis of such "tangible" factors as length of experience within the school district and the number of college "units" which teachers can manage to accumulate in summer sessions at the university, for all the world like housewives shopping for green stamps. This is like paying an insurance salesman on the basis of how long he has been with the company and how many courses in salesmanship he took in college.

The assumption is that taking summer courses and staying on one job for years automatically should qualify you for more pay than newer and younger teachers who haven't been around as long as you have.

Bunk.

Teaching is an art, the most ancient and incomparably most important art known to man. And we don't reward an artist on the basis of how long he has been hanging around the studio or how many art courses he took at dear old Random U.

As long as the teachers are brought closely and intimately

into the planning and the administration of merit pay, it is perfectly practicable.

I know. I've taught in districts which did just that. It worked like a charm.

THE EIGHTH LABOR
The Problem of Lifelong Teacher Tenure

In my last book on education, the chapter on teacher tenure is titled "The Protector of the Poor." In far too many places today that is exactly what tenure is.

In almost any calling or profession, a choice has to be made sooner or later between maximum freedom and maximum security. The two are fundamentally incompatible and the tendency of late has been to select the latter in preference to the former. There is nothing wrong with reasonable job security for teachers; there is everything wrong with making it the be-all and the end-all of education.

In every school district I've worked in, the best and most successful teachers were always the ones least interested in latching onto lifelong tenure. On the other hand, the weak sisters—and brothers—and those who were scared stiff of their ability to justify their own employment, were the very ones most sensitive and most resistant to any attempt to change the iron-clad tenure laws by so much as one comma.

Their excuse for such roadblocking was the danger which the profession always conjures up of the sinister, moustache-twisting school administrator victimizing the hapless and helpless instructor, firing him on trumped-up charges and turning him out into the snowy night, for all the world like the cruel father in Act 2 of "East Lynne." And I guess it has always been true in education, as it is in any other occupation, that even a gifted teacher could be fired by an arbitrary school superintendent or by a vindictive school board member.

During the bleak days of the Great Depression, a teacher's life was not a happy one. There were several teaching candidates for every teaching job, for one thing. If old Miss Smith kept Willy Jones after school for being impudent, or flunked him for refusing to do his home work, then an indignant Mr. Jones might decide to run for the school board so that he could avenge the family honor by firing Miss Smith. Every so often this would happen and poor Miss Smith would be on her way to the apple-selling business or the soup kitchen, things being rather tough all over in those days.

Not any more. Times have changed, with a vengeance. Today, the good teacher couldn't care less about the perils implicit in such a melodramatic situation. With teachers in chronically short supply, all the good teacher has to do to get a better job than the one from which Mr. Jones is trying to get her fired is to go almost literally around the corner and put in an application.

Where does this leave tenure? As I have said, "protector of the poor."

In my state you have to get a Superior Court judge to concur before a tenure teacher can be fired. Other states have similar laws. This is asinine. A judge may and probably does know as little about education as I know about jurisprudence. To make him the final arbiter of a teacher's destiny is as mutton-headed as it would be to ask him to pass on the competence of a nuclear physicist.

Such a procedure is silly and completely unprofessional. The vast majority of tenure teachers are the salt of the earth. They are hardly likely to be ill-treated by a school administration, any more than a gold mine or an oil well is apt to be ill-treated.

Still, we do turn up a real lemon now and then. Even law and medicine have their occasional shysters and quacks. When this happens in my line of work, we need machinery to enable us to police our own ranks as the doctors and the lawyers police theirs.

Few school board members or administrators have the time or the inclination to sit through prolonged court proceedings just to get rid of a teacher. The practical effect of this kind of a tenure law is that no tenure teachers get terminated in my state for any reason at all. In 99 cases out of 100 this works out fine, but if you happen to have a child enrolled in a class taught by that hundredth teacher, the problem will be just as real and agonizing for you as if that class were multiplied by a million.

In California we are working through our legislature to get our existing tenure laws modified to set up regional committees of eminent educators in each county to meet and counsel with local school boards which are trying to cope with the headache posed by the occasional incompetent teacher who somehow managed to qualify for tenure years ago and who is now hanging on grimly and frightenedly to a job nobody wants him to have.

It is not a question of trying to scuttle tenure. It is a question of trying to professionalize it.

THE NINTH LABOR
The Danger of Federal Aid to Education

Ever since the 1930s politicians and educators have been climbing into legislative beds with one another at odd intervals in order to push generalized federal aid to local education.

Until 1965 they were held at bay by odd combinations of forces, including school segregation in the South, Catholic demands for equal aid in the North and a poorly articulated but nonetheless genuine unease about federal control of the schools which permeated not only the North and the South, but the East and West as well.

But in 1965, Congress finally held its nose and took the plunge. Generalized federal aid to education slid through with little fuss and even less opposition, perhaps because it was cleverly disguised as something else.

There are two kinds of federal aid. One is itemized, earmarked money for certain specific projects vital to the national need. This kind of aid is older even than the Republic itself. It dates back to the Ordinance of 1787, which set aside plots of land for schools in every township of the vast Northwest Territory.

Other examples of specific aid are the Morrill Act of Lincoln's administration, which set up America's system of land grant colleges, and the G.I. Bill of the 1940s. No one seriously objects to this kind of federal aid, strictly limited to exceptional enterprises which are for one reason or another impossible to finance on a local or even a state level.

But the kind of federal aid most people think of is the multi-billion-dollar kind which brings Uncle Sam into the local school picture with both feet, barging into such non-specific and generally fuzzy areas as salaries and construction. This is the particular Pandora's Box, redolent with threats of national control and an end to grassroots government, which the recent Federal Aid to Elementary and Secondary Education Bill has now opened.

For instance:

It provides that school districts will get federal money on the basis of how many poor children are going to school there.

Note the two assumptions implicit in this provision. One is that a poor kid automatically needs government money for his education just because he *is* poor and hence bound to be culturally deprived. Such an assumption would certainly have amused such ex-poor kids as Abe Lincoln, Tom Edison, Henry Ford and quite a few others who managed to do all right both for themselves and for their country without any noticeable federal aid.

The other assumption is even weirder. It is the assumption that because a school district enrolls some children whose parents happen to be earning less than $2000 or in some cases $3000 per year, the district itself must therefore be poor as Job's turkey and in need of government money to run a decent educational program.

To my own certain knowledge, this assumption is a lot of baloney.

I used to work for a school system which was loaded

with utility money and needed federal aid about the same way Lyndon Johnson needs more publicity. Yet federal aid is exactly what it is going to get under the new law.

Why?

Because it happens to have quite a number of pupils whose parents are chronic reliefers and poverty cases, that's why.

So the wealthy school district, flush with its own tax money, is now going to get quite a lot of your money which it doesn't need because some of its pupils happen to come from poor families.

You don't believe it? Well, Beverly Hills qualified for an allocation of more than $50,000, and you know how miserable and poverty-stricken that poor city is. How many other school districts in my own state and yours are going to be in the same poignant predicament with your money? I do not know. But I do know that when I raised this objection in letters to congressmen and senators just before the new bill slid smoothly through, it was completely ignored.

If I were to put my finger on the biggest objection of all to this kind of federal aid, however, it would have to be through the medium of a perhaps-apocryphal story.

Prior to World War II, it was popularly rumored that the French minister of education entertained visitors to his Paris office by handing them a textbook, pointing to a clock on the wall and remarking: "If you will open to page 132, messieurs, you may read the second paragraph along with every single pupil in this grade in the entire French empire, for that is what all of them are doing at this very moment."

This is centralized, governmental education with a vengeance. Its evils are apparent. But not apparent enough, evidently. Witness the current trend toward massive, generalized federal aid, which always in the long run leads to massive federal control.

THE TENTH LABOR
God in the Schools

It is an open question whether the actual Supreme Court decisions are outlawing the very mention of God in the nation's schools or whether this result is stemming from some of the more eager-beaverish interpretations of those decisions by local authorities.

I personally incline toward the latter theory. But there is no question that a trend is running in this direction, sparked originally by the Vashti McCollum case back in the Thirties and accelerated by a whole string of related verdicts more recently.

As a result, I am informed that in New York the following lines cannot legally be spoken in the public schools:

"Then conquer we must, when our cause it is just,
And this be our motto: 'In God is our trust.'
And the Star-Spangled Banner in triumph shall wave
O'er the land of the free and the home of the brave."

In my own state demands have been served on several local school boards to outlaw all prayers, no matter whether they are spoken or sung. This poses a pretty problem for me, inasmuch as the state music books which my office distributes to our thousands of schools are chock full of prayers.

The irony of this whole situation comes from the fact that education in this country sprang directly from the needs of religion. With the Protestant Reformation of the 16th century, the followers of Luther and Calvin were expected to read and interpret the Scriptures for themselves. This was the attitude of the Pilgrim Fathers when they taught their children to read from the "hornbook primers" during those first bleak winters in New England. It was the attitude of their immediate descendants who wrote the "Old Deluder Satan" Act which first set up a system of publicly supported elementary schools in the Massachusetts Bay Colony.

Herein lies the paradox.

Public education, originally founded in our land to bulwark and interpret religion, is today forbidden to do anything of the sort. Today, education is commanded to teach not one group nor one caste or one sect, but all.

And since that "all" includes children of non-Christian and indeed nonreligious parents, the use of the school for religious purposes has entered of late upon a sharp and precipitate decline which has brought us to the point where the singing of Christmas carols has come under attack and where graduation baccalaureate services are having increasingly to be held off the high school campus altogether.

The reaction has obviously overcompensated. Everyone knows that public school teachers must not indulge in preaching or trying to interpret the Bible. There is no place for sectarian religion in our public schools. But there is still, it seems to me, a very important place for God in the nation's schools—not a Protestant God, nor a Catholic

God, nor a Jewish God, but God the common Father of us all.

In a nation founded largely for religious purposes, with God's name in its national anthem and its pledge of allegiance, with prayers to that same Deity rising each day from the chambers which shelter its Senate and its House of Representatives, it is incomprehensible to me that the little kindergarteners in my home town should now suddenly be forbidden by legal edict to say their simple thanks to their Creator for their daily cups of milk.

If you tell me that this sort of thing is what the Founding Fathers were thinking about when they wisely wrote the principle of separation of church and state into the Constitution, I tell you in return that you are talking blatant nonsense.

Religion and Education are forever linked together. Can history be taught minus the Rise of Christianity? Can art survive the loss of the Sistine Chapel, of Raphael's Madonnas? Can music tolerate the amputation of the magnificent canticles of our Judaeo-Christian heritage? Can literature, indeed, be taught at all without religion?

There is a trend running, like a river underground, and I don't like it. In a time when our national morals are at a record low, when our crime and juvenile delinquency rates have become objects of shuddering horror to the rest of the world, we need more moral and spiritual values in our schools, not fewer.

And you just can't duck the fact that there are no spiritual values without God.

The Golden State adopts and distributes its own textbooks, and every public school pupil has to use them, with no ifs, ands or buts. As a result, everything in these books is thus state-mandated. And in the past, I almost hesitate to report, there have been music books with lines like these:

"Our fathers' God, to Thee, author of liberty.
To Thee we sing.
Long may our land be bright with freedom's holy light;
Protect us by Thy might, great God our King."
                    and
"America, America, God shed His grace on thee."
                    and even
"God bless America, land that I love."

Let's face it. All these songs, and quite a few more like them, are prayers. And state-mandated prayers, at that.

Yes, siree. There we Californians stood with egg all over our faces, confronted with the unpalatable alternatives of either wiping much of our rich national musical heritage out of our books or telling the Supreme Court to go take a flying jump in the Pacific.

Well, we cut the Gordian Knot in our state and adopted some brand new music books. Take a look at some of the songs our California youngsters are now singing: "O, Come All Ye Faithful," "Away in a Manger," "O Hanukah," "Columbia the Gem of the Ocean," "The Stars and Stripes Forever" and even George M. Cohan's "You're a Grand Old Flag."

Yes, the great old songs are still there, and with them some mighty fine new ones. And yes, technically, some of them are undoubtedly written in the form of prayers.

But given the choice between a literal enforcement of an impossible court decision on the one hand and salvaging the warp and woof of America's musical birthright on the other, we've come out in favor of the latter.

If somebody wants to haul us into court, I guess we're ready for the paddy wagon. Singing merrily as we go.

Several of us are currently practicing a close harmony rendition of the "Battle Hymn of the Republic." A lot of brave gentlemen went into battle with its words on their lips a century ago and "died to make men free." The least we can do is to belt out a few choruses while we're being mugged and printed.

Who knows? We might even make the prison glee club.

THE ELEVENTH LABOR
The Puzzle of De Facto Segregation

The trouble with the puzzle of racial imbalance in the schools is that it is *in* education, but not *of* it.

It springs from incredibly complex and ancient causes, none of them educational in origin. It has its roots in trends largely beyond the ability of education to control. Yet there is the nagging certainty that the key to the long-range solution of de facto segregation lies in education and in education alone.

The danger that faces the schools today is that they will find themselves being used as a short-range rather than a long-range tool to solve the puzzle.

Cries are going up on all sides to end the time-tested concept of the neighborhood school, to bus certain arbitrary percentages of Negro and white children miles away across huge cities, over roaring freeways, through crowded industrial areas, in order to create in given schools for a few hours each day an artificial ratio of Negroes to whites.

In California we have had for years a special bureau under the direction of one of the nation's leading Negro educators. It is this bureau's duty to help local school districts deal with the distracting and perplexing problems summoned up by racial segregation. Every time its personnel have been called in to help solve such a problem, they have succeeded. And their watchword is: "Never try to suggest a solution to a school's racial problem which is immediately expedient but *educationally* unsound."

As do other states, California has schools which are almost completely segregated. It is not the schools, however, which are at fault in this matter. The great tide of Negro immigration into California after the war found itself largely funneled into segregated neighborhoods.

Because of man's inhumanity to man, because of the refusal of certain Americans to sell or to rent housing to certain other Americans, because of the inability of most Negroes to get decent jobs so that in turn they could afford decent homes, neighborhoods become all black or all white, and the schools as usual faithfully reflect the makeup of the neighborhoods for which they had been created years before.

There are ways to solve the puzzle. Schools can redraw attendance zones. They can plan new buildings on boundaries between all-white and all-Negro neighborhoods, drawing pupils from both. They can try such experimental proposals as specialized high schools, bringing pupils together from all parts of a large area on the basis of their curriculum majors and their special interests.

More recently I recommended educational "flight pay" —bonuses to persuade the best and finest teachers rather than the poorest and newest to work in the racial slums. We are bending every effort to see that the same principle is followed in assigning supplies, equipment and permanent installations to the less-favored socio-economic areas.

All these things are educationally sound. But we draw the line at unsound solutions. One of these is compulsory busing. A man should have the right to send his kids to school in his own neighborhood if he wants to. Maybe that was one big reason he invested in a home and moved into that particular neighborhood in the first place. But, there are some other pretty good arguments for the neighborhood school idea.

What happens to extracurricular activities and things like staying after school to get a little special help from the teacher when a certain arbitrary percentage of the pupils have to get on the bus as soon as the last bell rings every afternoon and take that long trip across town in order to get home at a decent hour?

What happens to parent-teacher conferences and PTA attendance and a host of related things when the home and the school are separated by substantial distances?

No, a man has the right to send his children to school in his own neighborhood. But he has no right under the sun to try to prevent other parents from sending their children to his neighborhood school if there is room in it, if the other parents want their children bused and if the elected school board feels that this is the way they want to operate.

So in California we are recommending voluntary busing when the climate and the distances are right. To some children and to some parents the advantages of attending a racially integrated school are so overridingly great that the disadvantages attendant upon busing are automatically relegated to a position of secondary importance. They should have the same right to send their children away that other parents have to keep their children close to home.

But in the long run, these are short-range remedies, palliative in nature.

Instead of allowing itself to be drawn into sterile and unproductive arguments as to how these things are to be implemented, it seems to me that education's main attention should be focused upon the main problem which it alone can solve: the inculcation, in the minds and hearts of the generation now growing up around us, of the American principles of tolerance and equality of opportunity which alone can ultimately defeat de facto segregation.

THE TWELFTH LABOR
The Teaching of Patriotism

In none of the other great labors facing education is there such a wide divergence of opinion and such a plethora of emotion as there is in the question of how patriotism should be taught in the public schools.

It is here, of course, that we are most vulnerable. Let one

generation grow up knowing nothing of John Smith and Pocahontas, John Alden and Priscilla Mullen, and the magic chain which links the future to the past is broken. The boys and girls grow up strangers to the great folk legends of the land: Washington and the cherry tree, Abe Lincoln and the borrowed book, "Black-Jack" Pershing and "Lafayette, we are here!"

The grand old sayings fade into the mists of yesterday, embalmed perhaps for future scholars but gone forever from the hearts and memories of the people:

"Now, indeed, we must all hang together, or most assuredly we shall all hang separately."

"Millions for defense, but not one cent for tribute!"

"Surrender? Why, sir, I have not yet begun to fight."

"With malice toward none, with charity for all . . ."

These are the things—these and a thousand more—which have made and preserved us a nation, which cluster together in a red, white and blue mist out of our past so that wide-eyed children will always remember. Farragut in the shrouds at Mobile Bay, Teddy Roosevelt at San Juan Hill, Dolley Madison saving the portrait of Washington, Betsy Ross and the first flag.

Without the great hero-stories, we are left in the schools with statistics on immigration and economic development, dry-as-dust treaties and proclamations, accounts of population trends and antitrust legislation to give the children in the guise of history. They will grow up inevitably with the same amount of love and reverence for their native land which they would feel for a mathematical theorem or a chemical formula. This, in the second half of the twentieth century, is just not good enough.

The lines which follow were once known by every school child in the country. They were a vital link in that chain of which I spoke. Try them on the children in your neighborhood if you want first-hand, personal proof of what 25 years of "life adjustment" "progressive" education have done to our historical heritage:

> "Ay, tear her tattered ensign down.
> Long has it waved on high.
> And many a heart has danced to see
> That banner in the sky."

and

> "By the rude bridge that arched the flood,
> Their flag to April's breeze unfurled,
> Here once the embattled farmers stood,
> And fired the shot heard round the world."

and

> "The breaking waves dashed high
> On a stern and rock-bound coast."

It may be argued that mere mouthing of rhymed couplets and the parroting of phrases from great speeches will do nothing to instill in our children an understanding of our nation's past and an abiding faith in her future. And this is true to the same extent that reciting the wedding vows will do little in itself to insure a happy marriage. But few of us would feel genuinely married without this moving spiritual experience at the outset of our voyage across the perilous sea of matrimony.

Even so is the case of the great stories and poems and speeches which summarize so eloquently and so dramatically the adventures of the American people down through the centuries. We commit a crime not only against the child but also against the country itself when we remove these grand reminders of yesterday from the curriculum of today.

I charge that our enchantment with "social studies" and "social living" instead of history has taken us a long way down the road to oblivion.

I charge also that our current reluctance openly and proudly to voice our belief in the greatness and goodness of our country is causing the children to believe that patriotism is corny.

What have we done to ourselves by abandoning to random political groups the precious birthright of every American to love his country and to say so?

Where does this sick, shamefaced philosophy leave the schools?

How can we transmit the precious heritage of the past to the citizens of the future?

The schools alone will be helpless to remedy this evil. It will take the united efforts of all of us to make it acceptable and even fashionable once again to love our country and to say so before all men.

The schools must be a witness to the truth. And the truth is that this is the greatest and the freest and the finest country in the world. Somehow we must get this idea across to the kids.

The facts about the great sweep and drama of America's

past were enough for the children who grew up to be our grandparents. They will be enough for our grandchildren, too, if we can just be sure in the schools that the great story continues to be told.

Books and Reading

Books are the building blocks of education.

That is, if the pupils know how to read.

Even then, not ALL books used in schools these days are building blocks. Some of the more recent vintage would look more at home in a brothel.

CENSORSHIP IN THE SCHOOLS
Every teacher is a censor. And rightly so . . .

At a recent public gathering one of the more adrenal and less cerebral members of the audience pointed an accusing forefinger at me and barked: "Do you really believe in censoring what is taught in the schools?"

By dint of heroic and unaccustomed self-control, I refrained from telling my questioner exactly how fat-headed his query was and contented myself with a mild: "Yes, sir. Don't you?" This may not have been the most brilliant riposte in the world, but it had at least the twin virtues of brevity and forbearance.

For every schoolman practices censorship almost every day of his professional life. We have to. We may call it "screening," or "assignment of material at appropriate maturation levels," or some such fiddle-faddle, but it's censorship, nonetheless.

My dictionary defines a censor as "anyone who exercises supervision over manners and morals." If this doesn't describe one of the key roles of any teacher, I'll eat my mortarboard. The laws of every state in the Union, so far as I know, spell out in considerable detail the responsibility of the instructor in this vital area of public education, and rightly so.

We do not assign Gibbon's *Decline and Fall* to second graders. Rarely have I seen the memoirs of the Marquis de Sade or the clinical studies of Krafft-Ebbing on the shelves of high school libraries. The literature instructor who assigned *Fanny Hill* or *The Life and Loves of Frank Harris* to his ninth-grade class would probably not only get the sack, but also have his credential yanked.

Does anyone in his right mind seriously question not only the right but the positive duty of school people to exercise such judgment? We may camouflage it under the label of "selectivity" or "good taste," but what we are actually doing is saying that some material is suitable for children to study and to learn, and some is not.

The same principle holds in other areas of the curriculum. I would hesitate a long while before adopting a civics text authored by Boss Tweed.

The question often comes up: "But shouldn't children know about such points of view, wrong though they may be? Isn't this a part of life? Aren't we indoctrinating when we don't teach them everything?"

I feel about this much as I feel about assigning a book like *Catcher in the Rye* to a high school American literature class. Should it be assigned, and to whom?

Certainly it should be assigned—to those students who have read Homer and Virgil, who have laughed with Dickens and wept with Shakespeare, who have lived with and learned to love the great American writers who have stood the test of time, from Philip Freneau to Mark Twain. Students grounded in the culture and the wisdom of the past are ready to judge and to evaluate what passes for the literature of the present.

Remember this: Just because a thing exists, it is not necessarily incumbent upon the school to serve it up to children any more than a physician is obligated to prescribe arsenic to a patient merely because it happens to be in the pharmacopoeia.

You ask who should decide what is good for children to study and what is not. And I reply that we educators should. This is what you hire us for. This is why we study many long and painful years to qualify ourselves. It is part of our job.

Those few members of my profession who welsh on their duty, who let down all bars of decency and morality, who serve up to the children placed in their care stones instead of bread are beneath contempt.

They betray us all.

SOMETIMES FICTION IS MORE REAL THAN TRUTH
Literature's only acid test is the test of time . . .

Judging from the mail I get these days, a lot of parents are getting pretty steamed over some of the so-called "avant-garde" literature currently being assigned their offspring in high school. Such modern classics as *Lord of the Flies* and *Catcher in the Rye* are under especially heavy fire.

"It's ridiculous and revolting to ask children to read downbeat novels like these," fumes one choleric correspondent. "They're nothing but dreadful, dreary recitals of sickness, sordidness and sadism."

This is certainly a legitimate criticism, although candor compels me to admit that it is one which could also be made of other belles-lettres than ours today. Few modern writers, for example, can hold a scatological candle to Dan Chaucer at his filthiest, and our own American original, Poe, surely wasn't the healthiest and least morbid of authors, by a long shot.

But this is not my own objection to present-day literature. I do not happen to think it is literature, which my dictionary defines as "written works dealing with themes of permanent and universal interest, characterized by creativeness and grace of expression."

Leaving grace of expression out of it completely, because I haven't seen any of it for so long, let us talk about creativeness for a moment.

One of the tests of a real writer in any age is his ability to create, out of paper and ink, living, breathing characters who walk abroad in the land and dwell abidingly in the minds and hearts of men. Truly great literature will animate such towering prototypes that they become part of both the folklore and the verbal currency of entire peoples.

Such a figure is Homer's Odysseus, whose interminable and wily wanderings evoked a 2500-year school of picaresque fiction and added the common noun "odyssey" to a dozen languages.

Another is the roistering, irreverent Falstaff. Shakespeare's protuberant sack-swiller is more alive today than he was in 1600. He even lends his name to a modern alcoholic brew, a logical twist which would have gladdened the hearts of certain Mermaid Tavern habitués three centuries ago.

More recently, a lean, hawk-faced private eye named Holmes made London's Baker Street famous, inspired whole schools and swarms of imitators and gave his first name to popular parlance forevermore as a synonym for the word "detective."

Quickly, now, without delving into the glossaries and anthologies, name me some comparable folk-figures who have emerged from all the incredible spate of writing which has cascaded upon us since World War II.

How about a modern Micawber? A contemporary Count of Monte Cristo? A present-day Peter Pan?

I don't see any. Do you? Always excepting the ineffable James Bond, of course.

This is why I have some king-size reservations about a lot of the books currently being passed off as modern literature.

And please don't try to tell me that I am being unduly impatient and that future generations will eventually immortalize the drably anonymous non-heroes of our current sex sagas. I just don't believe it. It did not take long for the Elizabethans to appreciate Ariel or the Victorians to embrace Tom Sawyer.

So if I were teaching high school English today as I taught it for more than 20 years I would try to make very sure that my students had been made thoroughly aware of the time-tested titans of our great literary past before I exposed them to the admittedly unproved fictioneers of the flickering, uncertain present.

First things first. Especially with children.

After all, it is only familiarity with the great writing of the ages which will give America's youngsters the judgment and the discretion to deal with what passes for the literature of the future.

Or the stomach, for that matter.

POISON FREE WITH A CARD
*I love librarians, but some of them don't seem
to realize the dynamite they're dealing
with . . .*

The librarians in my state got together in a convention recently and managed to come up with one of the most irresponsible statements I've heard in some time.

"There is no evidence," one of them assured his peers in solemn convocation, "that anybody ever committed a crime as the result of having read a book."

Oh, brother!

Usually the information media unearth stories like this to feature at the height of the so-called Silly Season, which normally comes around each August, when people are pretty well played out and ready to grin tolerantly at almost any story which will help take their minds off the hot weather. But for librarians to make a statement like this in December seems to be rushing the Silly Season.

Every law enforcement officer in the land knows the high probability of finding pornographic books among the personal effects of minors picked up for sex crimes, and the grislier the crime, the higher the probability.

If the librarians want to argue the matter of cause and effect, what about the news story which came out about a week after their little get-together, quoting a youthful perpetrator of a particularly ghastly murder who conceded that he had been inspired to commit it by reading the memoirs of the Marquis de Sade?

If memory serves me right, one Gilles de Retz back in the days of Joan of Arc slaughtered platoons of girls and little children, to get their blood for certain revolting experiments based on instructions included in various books on black magic. It was shortly after this that he was given the nickname by which he is known to us today: Bluebeard.

We do not have to go back to the 15th century for examples of bad books instigating bad actions, however. In our own time, I'm sure even the librarians will recall a book entitled *Mein Kampf*. Its bloody advice was followed to the letter not only by its psychopathic author, but also by an entire nation, which for 12 years used it as a bible of destruction. The crimes it motivated have not passed from the world scene even to this day.

There is no greater instrumentality for influencing human conduct than a book. Whether for good or for ill, we erring mortals are conditioned to believe what we read on a printed page. And those printed words can overthrow great nations and change the course of history. From the Talmud to *Uncle Tom's Cabin* the evidence is crystal clear for those with eyes to see.

What distresses me is the apparent inability of my friends the librarians to see what everyone else sees. Oh, I know what they are driving at. They are trying to fend off irresponsible censorship which might reduce them to the status of mere robots moving spasmodically among out-of-bounds book stacks and brandishing futile date stamps.

But trying to kid the public into believing that books are

incapable of inspiring either crime or the cardinal virtues is simply flying in the face of the entire history of the human race, at least since the Egyptians invented hieroglyphics.

Librarians are among our most important public servants, for in their hands lies the great legacy of the past. What they ought to be doing is devising professional ways to supply books to children based alike upon maturity, propriety and plain common sense.

No one in a responsible position wants to start censoring books intended for adults only. But if librarians or anyone else think the American public is going to sit idly by and watch filth and corruption made available for children at the taxpayers' expense, they have another think coming.

WHAT'S WRONG WITH SIMPLIFICATION?
A word on behalf of simplicity. In teaching reading, anyhow . . .

In the game of schoolmanship, one of the earmarks of a true pro is to accuse his critics of oversimplifying the issues. Such a charge is virtually guaranteed to land the would-be censurers in the Slough of Simplification, wallowing about hopelessly, spluttering from time to time that they do perceive the true complexities of education in the 20th century, honestly they do.

Thus, when someone makes the suggestion that children be taught to read by memorizing the 26 letters of the alphabet and the various sounds attached to them and then putting them together into syllables—those indispensable building blocks of the language—the riposte of the so-called methodology expert is first to smile gently at the simplicity of the suggestion. Second he elaborates on the research done on the "configuration-contour" or "look-say" method of teaching reading during the past 20 years. Finally he expresses regret that the critic has seen fit to advocate methods which have been hopelessly outdated by the increasing complexities of modern existence.

The phonics advocate who lets himself be put on the defensive by this sort of gambit deserves his fate. His proper course is to remind his subtle insulter that life may become more complicated, but kids don't, and that the rules of reading have not been altered over the centuries by the invention of spaceships, steam engines, gas balloons or the Macedonian phalanx, for that matter.

He then clings grimly to the jugular of the issue, citing the horrendous growth both of "remedial reading" classes on all levels of education and the so-called "Bonehead English" courses set up by our colleges to teach the basic fundamentals of the mother tongue to freshmen who should have mastered them long before the fifth grade.

Our critic then would do well to lift a page from the devil's own handbook, quoting the gospel according to St. John Dewey to the effect that in education we judge pragmatically and strictly in accordance with how a given practice or theory works.

Obviously the "look-say" Egyptian hieroglyphic method of teaching reading hasn't worked worth a plugged nickel, or we would not after two decades and more still be so concerned about raising a generation of quasi-illiterates.

Usually at this moment of the debate, the embattled

phonics upholder looks around for his opponent and finds to his surprise that he is alone in the ring. His Progressive Education adversary has sneaked out between the ropes and is busy in another part of town organizing a "workshop" for other methodology experts at which they will pass resolutions congratulating themselves upon their success nationwide in resisting extremist attempts to oversimplify the reading problem.

It seems to me that for every attempt to oversimplify something these days there are a dozen efforts to make complex mountains out of originally uncomplicated mole-hills. It is not that hard to teach kids to read. In fact, any healthy youngster above the low-grade moron level can learn his letters and how to put them together if he is taught with a minimum of nonsense.

The same principle, incidentally, applies to other sectors of the educational battlefield. A lot of guidance boils down to teaching a child the difference between right and wrong, and for this the counselor does not have to spend half a lifetime studying Freud and Jung.

English grammar hasn't changed much, either, in the last century or so, except that fewer people know about it. The intricacies of the Nuclear Age have not repealed its laws of sentence structure, verb conjugations and punctuation. What grammar needs most right now is not new method-ology, but a supply of teachers who understand it and are willing to teach it.

Curriculum has overproliferated. We could do a lot of good by cutting out a few courses such as "The Home and the Community," "The County and its Industries," "Stu-dent Leadership," "Ninth Grade Social Studies" and so on and on. If it be oversimplifying to cull this niggling trivia, so be it.

There is nothing especially complex about the "Ten Commandments" or the "Sermon on the Mount" or the "Gettysburg Address." Most of the great guides to human conduct which light up the past like beacons in a stormy night have been the quintessence of simplicity.

And so, despite its necessary but peripheral trappings of complexity, should be the inner glow of education.

Children

Kids are education's main reason for existence.

This doesn't prevent them from causing educators to climb the walls from time to time.

A GRAIN OF SALT
*Sometimes you need the whole
darned salt-cellar . . .*

"Oh, it ain't necessarily so . . ."

This may come as a shock to mothers, but Junior does not always tell the truth; especially about what goes on at school.

He will not often come home and deliberately lie. It's just that frequently he and the school are operating on different wave lengths. He functions within one frame of reference, and teacher is working within quite another one. For instance:

A rather large and highly indignant mom complained to the school principal about me one day some years ago. It seems that I had sent her son home from school for disrupting the institutional decorum.

"And all Neddy said," she concluded triumphantly, "was 'Yes sir.'"

Charged with this act of apparently senseless brutality, I had to admit to the puzzled principal that all Neddy had indeed said was "Yes sir." What he hadn't told his mother was that he had said it in the school library during a study hall, after previously being told to pick up 12 books which he had purposely knocked off the shelves and onto the floor. He had said it in a roar which reverberated around the campus and would have done credit to old Stentor himself.

Another hot-eyed parent recently demanded the hide of young Miss Jones because she had insulted Mary Smith in front of the entire class.

"I know my Mary isn't the slimmest girl in the school," Mrs. Smith quavered pathetically," "but that doesn't give her teacher the right to call her an elephant!"

"An elephant?" queried the horrified administrator.

"And a sturdy elephant at that!" trumpeted Mother.

Poor Miss Jones at first denied all knowledge of the crime. Finally, after racking her memory, light broke.

"I've certainly never called one of my pupils an elephant," she stated gently but firmly, "but I do recall having to scold Mary the other day for being a disturbing *element*."

In neither of these cases did the children lie. Neddy told the exact truth but not all of it, and Mary told what she thought the teacher had said but got it all wrong. In each instance, Mom was crouched at home waiting with quivering antennae for someone at "that school" to get out of line at the expense of *her* child. She never bothered to get the teacher's side of the question.

Don't get me wrong. We teachers are often guilty of error in such matters, and when we are we deserve to get called on the carpet. But we resent being condemned automatically on the word of one of our pupils, who admittedly is both immature and ignorant. Otherwise he wouldn't be in school.

Unfortunately, educators are apparently the easiest people in the world to misunderstand—and not just by children. The other day, a lady called me in a cold rage. She had heard a tape of a talk I had given, and according to her I had been beastly to a religious minority, namely the Buddhists. This baffled me. I don't even know any Buddhists.

The lady insisted and finally hung up rather violently. I sat there brooding. Finally I exhumed a dusty copy of the old speech and went through it word for word. Sure enough, at the bottom of page three I found that I had indeed been highly critical of a modern disciplinary phenomenon—the leatherjacketed, *booted* slob.

What can I say? To that lady, I will always be the man to whom all Buddhists are slobs. When she hung up, you see, she didn't leave her number.

A CHILD'S MIND IS UNKNOWN TERRITORY
The two worlds of the teacher . . .

> *"Childhood's joyland—mystic, merry Toyland—*
> *Once you pass its borders, you can ne'er return again . . ."*
>
> VICTOR HERBERT

When you come upon your touslehead pulling the wings off flies or setting fire to the cat, does this mean he's sadistic?

Of course it does.

When Susie knows you're sad and dejected and offers to

stay home from the birthday party to keep you company because "she loves you so," does this mean she's a saint?

Naturally.

And when five-year-old Billy talks to invisible animal friends who follow him around the yard, does this mean he's nuts?

To a certain extent.

Actually, all of us at any age turn upon the world in rapid succession the masks of the sadist, the saint and the psychotic. But as we grow older we tend to supress increasingly and express decreasingly both the fiendish and the angelic facets of our hopelessly divided natures, until by the time senility has set in we have become incurable hypocrites.

A hypocritical child, however, is a contradiction in terms, and thus almost unknown. So we can observe real human nature by studying its overt symptoms in the very young, but we can go badly awry if we regard Junior as merely an undeveloped daddy.

Teaching is the most rewarding and frustrating of callings. Why? Because teachers have to live in two worlds at the same time.

One is the adult world of automation and anxiety, ultrasonics and ulcers, deficits and deals. And I suppose we educators are as reasonably at home in this squirrel cage as anyone can claim to be.

The other is the strange, distorted, half-world of childhood, shot through in equal parts with passionate hopes and desperate fears, simultaneously lighted by the lamps of love and clouded by the crepuscles of cruelty. And here we find ourselves in an uncharted terra incognita, with only notoriously unreliable memories of our own childhoods for maps.

It is easy and somehow comforting for grownups to assume that the mind of a child is simply a miniature version of the mind of a man and that, therefore, a child is just a tiny adult, a kind of midget with a growth potential. Our forebears back in the 17th and 18th centuries carried this whopping non sequitur to its logical conclusion by actually dressing their eight-year-olds in doubtlets and hose and three-cornered hats.

But a child is not a little man. He is a being in transition and a lot closer to the raw simplicities of the primeval jungle than any of us will ever be again or than we like to think we ever were. Childhood may be mystic, as Victor Herbert said, but it's often very far from merry.

For one thing, the child lives in a world where both time and space are vastly different from ours. A year to a child may easily be a week to us. A bungalow to us six-footers is a skyscraper to him, a wooded grove the limitless forests of Xanadu.

He is notably impatient where we have learned patience. He is openly and candidly selfish where we have been pressured by the needs of society to conceal our own self-interest. He is direct where we are devious, simple where we prefer to be complicated.

Nothing outrages a child more than unfairness, no matter how glossed-over or rationalized. We adults are accustomed to it and practice it as a matter of course, a contorted commentary on the merits of maturity.

Above all, a child is perennially and pryingly curious. Curiosity is his badge and symbol and does more than any other quality to set him off, alien and apart, from the world of adulthood.

So it is that we who practice the immemorially ancient art of teaching must learn first to follow John Stuart Mill's advice to think in different terms. The raw material we deal with is so vastly different from the finished product we aspire to that it often seems that we educators are trying feverishly and devotedly to transform one species into another and profoundly incompatable one, within the space of 12 to 16 years.

Remember this the next time you feel called upon to voice the timeless complaint about a teacher: "He just doesn't understand my child!"

Does anyone?

Has anyone, I wonder, ever really understood a child?

REJECTION IS A HIGHLY RELATIVE THING
*The kids really don't have it half as bad
as they like to think . . .*

I have the gloomiest of forebodings that I am going to be grossly misunderstood. Worse yet, I may be branded the Scroogest of curmudgeons by any of my juvenile friends who chance to read this.

Ah, well. 'Twas ever thus for those who tilt at windmills. And this particular windmill is the universally accepted myth of the Byronically misunderstood adolescent, nobly defiant in a wicked world he never made.

My friends among the psychologists and sociologists may and do disagree on nearly everything else these days, but they join hands as happily as the Vassar daisy chain in calling today's teen-agers the "rejected generation." The kids are alienated, they say. All lines of communication between oldsters and youngsters are short-circuited as never before and are, in fact, about to burn out completely.

And who's to blame?

Come off it. Who's always to blame? The parents, of course.

They are too immersed in their heated swimming pools, too absorbed in keeping up with the Joneses, too submerged in the banalities of *la dolce vita* to know or care what Junior is doing. The poor kid is cut adrift practically at puberty and left to his own hopeless devices.

A heart-rending picture is projected of Junior wandering aimlessly about the streets, pining lugubriously for the tender, loving, parental care he has never known and generally going to perdition along a highway mapped out and paved by Mom and Pop.

There are some cases like this. Quite a few, unfortunately, But then there always have been. The fact is that the vast majority of modern parents is just as affectionate, far better informed and vastly more concerned about their offspring than any other mothers and fathers in history. And if this be rank heresy, make the most of it.

What other generation ever had lavished upon it, like dollops of hot fudge, such a superabundance of pediatricians, vitamin supplements, hula hoops, Barbie dolls, Dr. Spock manuals and free college scholarships?

What panting parents have ever knocked themselves out so doggedly leading Boy Scout troops, umpiring Little League supercolossals, patronizing family counselors, officering PTAs and manning community recreation programs?

What other younglings in the annals of our planet ever got away with dictating clothing styles, calling the tune on popular music trends, setting and upsetting the ancient policies of great universities and in general making such shrill and querulous nuisances of themselves as these our children?

And to wax coldly commercial for the nonce, what other kids in all the world have ever had so much hard cash jingling in their pockets? Especially without doing any work to earn it.

This is rejection? What the devil do they have to feel alienated about? Too much affluence? Too much newspaper attention? Too much concern?

Could be.

But the kids didn't initiate this sniveling image of themselves. It has been built up for them during the past few years by adults who should have known better. By "experts" who got carried away by their own expertise.

If it will help make my point, let me conjure up some real swinging examples of past small fry who really *were* rejected.

Charles Dickens found himself farmed out to a blacking factory at the tender age of 11 and for the rest of his life woke up screaming from galloping nightmares.

Mark Twain, an orphaned 12-year-old, worked six days a week as a printer's apprentice for his room and keep.

And Andrew Carnegie, age 13, was slaving his little life away in a textile mill for the munificent sum of $1 per week.

Yes, other generations than our own have had alienated offspring. I guess the big difference is that we worry more about ours. And probably we worry more because there are more kids than ever before. In the 1970s half our nation's population will be under 25.

No, we haven't rejected our children. A lot of them have temporarily rejected us, true enough. So what else is new?

Sam Clemens once said: "When Joe was 16 he thought his father was an idiot. But when he turned 26 he was amazed to discover how much sense the old fellow had got in the last 10 years."

ARE WE WORKING THE KIDS TOO HARD THESE DAYS?
Nor, indeed, are they worked half as hard
as they think they are . . .

"Have we burned out a decade's supply of high school students by making them work too hard?"

The *Journal of the American Association for the Advancement of Science* recently asked this somewhat incendiary question, answered itself "Yes" and followed it up with its own reason for this mass immolation: too much homework.

The journal blames Sputnik and the "hysteria" which followed hard upon its intrusion into American sky-space for the present plight of our hapless teen-agers, condemned to endless toil in our academic sweatshops. It cites as evidence the recent disquieting warning of L. Carroll King, a professor of chemistry at Northwestern:

"By the time the student completes secondary school,

we have asked him to do too much, too fast, too soon and have asked him to keep at it too long."

Conscientious high school students may stagger through a horrendous 17-hour day, Dr. King cautions, and as a result become mere shells of their former selves.

"After four years of this, Mr. Good Student is a tired, discouraged old man. We have committed a crime against a generation."

Really, now! Let's not get carried away. Before we buy this particular version of the Apocalypse, let's subject it to the acid test of personal observation and experience, Socratic style.

Try these questions on for size, Mom and Pop:

1—Do your kids work 17 hours a day? At anything?

2—How many tired, discouraged old men do you number among your adolescent acquaintances?

3—When did you last meet an 18-year-old who was a burned-out, haggard shell?

And lest you complain that I'm playing dirty pool by confining you arbitrarily to your possibly limited circle of teen-age friends, permit me to bear personal witness that during a lifetime of daily contact with teen-agers of all shapes, sizes and colors I have never known one of them who answered even remotely to Dr. King's somewhat zombie-like description.

Have you?

This doesn't necessarily mean that there aren't any, of course. In fact, I'm prepared to admit that there are. A few. But I'm also prepared to argue that (1) there has always been a minority of young people who worked too hard, (2) there is no larger percentage of overworked adolescents today than there was back in the 1930s and (3) Sputnik had little or nothing to do with the whole thing.

Out of every typical batch of 100 normal kids there have always been about three or four at one end of the spectrum who burned the midnight oil inordinately, three or four at the other end who refused to burn any at all and roughly 92 in the middle who worked just hard enough to get B's, C's or D's, depending on their brain-power, will-power and general inclination to hit the books instead of scuba diving beneath the waves or riding surf boards on top of them.

This percentage hasn't changed noticeably in recent years.

When Sputnik first pre-empted our attention and loosened our purse strings for education, it did indeed touch off a long-overdue series of major reforms in the existing Mack Sennett melange of social studies, language arts, student leadership courses, personal grooming classes and senior problems seminars which passed for so much of the typical high school curriculum less than a decade ago.

Homework came back into its own after a quantitative hiatus of too many years. Grades became important once again. Togetherness, ingroupness and "life adjustment" lost some of their lure.

It was about time, too.

I can't say I share Dr. King's obvious alarm. Some kids get neurotic over their homework, I guess. But I'd a lot rather have them home late at night wrestling with logarithms and the table of elements than out taking "trips" in some pad or helling around with the local rat pack.

After all, you can always take them off homework. But how do you get them off LSD?

The Classroom

Subject matter is what education is all about.

How well we get it across is the only real test we teachers have to face up to.

But an awful lot of other things go on in class besides recitation and testing.

WHAT ARE THE FRILLS?
*Some folks think school frills are things like
home economics and music. They aren't . . .*

Every so often someone tees off on education's so-called "frills." Often these turn out to be architectural details which violate the critic's sense of seemliness and economy—things in the new school plant like swimming pools and faculty lounges.

Yet swimming is a lifelong skill, which is more than can be said of football and basketball, and it can save a life now and then, which is more than baseball and track can do.

And as for faculty lounges, even teachers like to sit down once in a while in pleasant surroundings and converse with their colleagues, a practice which dates back at least as far as Plato and Aristotle and would, I'm sure, have their hearty endorsement.

Sometimes frills are alleged in the field of curriculum, with such subjects as crafts and home economics and even instrumental music coming under the gun.

Yet the first two named are probably going to be of more lasting value and importance to more children than are geometry, algebra, Latin and ancient history put together, and music has been a part of the classical curriculum since the days of Pericles right down through the medieval quadrivium.

Obiously, if a school is impoverished and has to establish a subject priority list or go out of business, it is possible to do so. Some subjects are of such overriding importance that everything else has to take a back seat, relatively speaking.

Such a subject is English, which is the great prerequisite for everything else. Without mastery of its essentials, the historian cannot write his monographs or the astronomer describe his novas. The physicist is limited to mathematics and the biologist to color movies of fruit flies unless somewhere along the line they have been subjected to the discipline of the mother tongue.

But to say that some subjects are more important than others is a far cry from saying that the less important ones are necessarily frills.

Does this mean, then, that there are no frills at all in modern education?

By no means.

Such high school courses as ninth-grade "social studies" and twelfth-grade "senior problems" could profitably be dropped in favor of a year of freshman world geography and senior economics, respectively.

I doubt, either, if anyone would really miss courses like "student leadership" and "personal grooming," both of which are to be found not infrequently in the high schools of my state. Not that these subjects are evil or completely valueless. It's just that there are probably more important things to which the children need to be exposed.

Adult education has been widely condemned for devot-

ing too much time to things like cake decorating and up-
holstering, but people tend to lose sight of the fact that
such night classes are usually the result of popular demand
and are customarily paid for by tuition fees. Incidentally,
if they are not so financed, they ought to be.

I knew a school once that taught flycasting in its adult
education classes. It was on the Colorado River, the course
was eminently practical and the enrollees paid the entire
cost of the class. There's nothing wrong with this that I
can see.

What is a frill? It is something taught at public expense
which cannot be justified in terms of money spent and
pupil time involved when it is confronted with the acid
test of the following question: "Does it contribute signi-
ficantly and importantly to the development of the individual's maximum potential and to the survival of the
United States in the second half of the 20th century?"

THE NEW MATH
The new math can be pretty frustrating—
for parents . . .

Those of us with children in grade school are having some
traumatic experiences with home work these days, if we
happen to be living in states which are introducing something called "the new math."

Used to think you were pretty sharp in the mathematics
department, didn't you? What do you tell Junior now
when he comes home and asks for help with things called
"commutativity" and "algorisms"? Or do you just get mad

and tell off Junior's school for fooling around with this new-fangled jargon?

I know. It's frustrating enough to be a parent nowadays without having to cope with a whole new approach to something so enduring and immutable as math was supposed to be. But we have no choice. This is one revolution in which America must participate or forfeit its right to world leadership within a single generation.

You see, this is computer mathematics, spawned by the imperatives of the space age. It stresses underlying concepts rather than rote memorization of number combinations. It emphasizes base number systems, such as the binary mathematics around which most calculating machines are built, and teaches the children that our traditional decimal, or "base 10" system, is only one of many.

The new math is dedicated to the "why," but it includes all the old math's attention to the "how," as well. The multiplication tables still have to be learned—more completely than before, as a matter of fact, because the small fry need to be led to a more complete understanding of why multiplication takes place and to a knowledge of some of the other ways that can be used to arrive at the number 25 in addition to multiplying 5 times 5.

My home state recently adopted textbooks which are intended to act as a bridge between the old math and the new. There is always the danger that educational innovations of this kind may turn out to be gimmicks, but there is an even greater danger that educators may be so comfortable in their velvet-lined ruts that they ignore or oppose any departure from the status quo.

The new books are designed to follow Alexander Pope's admonition to "be not the first by whom the new are tried, nor yet the last to lay the old aside." They present to the youngsters the concept of "set," and the idea that printed or written numbers are merely symbols of sets, or collections of things. Yet they stress mastery of the basic processes, too.

It will be interesting to see what the future holds in this important member of the "Three R" trinity. First graders are going to be learning some of the underlying principles of algebra and geometry. Some high school students will doubtless be studying calculus. In no other field of instruction are things changing at so rapid a rate.

For those parents who fail to see the need for the new math, let me give one illustration.

In my day, plane geometry started out on the first day with an axiom so self-evident that proof was never required. This was that under whatever conditions prevailed, the shortest distance between two points was always a straight line. Remember?

Mom and Dad, I've got news for you. It isn't so any more. To astronauts like Col. Glenn and his colleagues, dealing with two points separated by almost inconceivable distances within the Einsteinian "curved universe," a curved line may very well be the shortest distance between them.

Makes you think, doesn't it? Not only about the new math, but about this strange, wonderful, new universe unfolding all about us these days like a cosmic panorama. The old, comfortable ways are no longer enough. The mere fact that we have been happy and at ease with the tools of the past is no justification whatever for our denying to the next generation the strange and glittering implements of the future.

THE DECLINE AND FALL OF LATIN
Quos Deus perdere vult, prius dementat . . .

We could lose a lot of things from the public school curriculum and never miss them: social studies, senior problems, ninth grade orientation, even "student leadership." But these are the very subjects which seem to hang on with a grim and maddening persistence, as hard to stamp out as crab grass.

Other subjects, alas, seem all too prone to vanish little by little over the years like the Cheshire Cat, leaving behind not even the ghost of a grin. Such a disappearing act is currently being done by the oldest item in the curriculum: Latin.

A wire service announcement early this year reported that 25% fewer schools are now teaching the language of Caesar and Cicero than were doing so a mere decade ago.

When you think about this seriously for even a moment, it figures.

For one thing, Latin is the parent tongue. Nearly all the great, productive, modern European languages are to a greater or lesser degree slang Latin—the idiom spoken by legate and centurion alike 2000 years ago as the clanking cohorts of Rome garrisoned the far-flung outposts of empire from Hadrian's Wall in Scotland to the Dacian frontier of today's Romania.

French, Spanish, Portuguese, Italian and a vast segment of English spring from the speech of old Rome and until our own philistine generation, were proud to call her "mere," "madre" and other similarly venial corruptions of the original "mater."

But we brave-new-worlders do not render very much respect unto parents any more, whether the parents be consanguine or linguistic. The ignorant arrogance of youth for mere youth's sake is increasingly in the saddle and riding off booted and spurred in all directions, as evidenced by the almost incredibly stupid statement being heard today on our more "avant-garde" college campuses: "Don't trust anybody over 30."

Applied literally and historically, of course, this addled adage would keep young people from listening to anyone who ever had anything worthwhile to say, from Christ to John Kennedy.

In such a raised-in-a-vacuum pseudo-intellectual environment as this, parents find themselves considered first squares, then cubes and finally complete nullities. So it is with the parent language, too.

But the decline and fall of Latin constitute a much more savage indictment of what we laughingly call our contemporary culture than that embodied in the familiar revolt of youth against age. The ancient tongue has for more than 20 centuries represented the supreme example of logic as applied to language.

The orderly declensions of its nouns, the methodical conjugations of its verbs have marched down the ages in laconic, no-nonsense majesty like the legions of Octavius, flanked on the right by the light cavalry of the ablative absolute and on the left by the slingers and archers of indirect discourse. Over the years, the rhetoric of the Forum and the grammar of the Senate have swept every semantic battlefield to which they have been challenged by the forces of linguistic corruption and verbal sloppiness.

Until our own time.

We have apparently elected to dry-gulch Latin the way Fabius the Delayer finally got rid of Hannibal. He couldn't beat his enemy in fair fight, and he refused to parley with him, so he just ignored him to death.

Every so often he would chop up the great conqueror's supply lines and cut off a few of his isolated scouting units, all the while never daring to look the formidable Carthaginian in the face. Eventually Hannibal's forces just eroded away, and this is precisely what is happening to Latin.

We have little place for logic in our society today, it seems. In our politics and air pollution, our law enforcement and our literature, our manners and our morals, logic is so conspicuous by its absence that a language based upon it is as out of place as a balanced budget in Washington.

For those of you who want your children trained in orderly and disciplined thinking, as well as conversant with the mother tongue of western Europe and the New World, however, let me urge you to bestir yourselves before it is too late.

The schools are still responsive to your wishes. I suggest you speak out, loudly and clearly and to the point, lest the creeping cancer of banality cancel out not only the grave beauty of antique Latin, but also eventually all that is glorious and grand and great in our own English, Latin's heir and beneficiary.

WHAT'S WRONG WITH ATHLETES?
To say nothing of "Mens sana in corpore sano" . . .

If there is one stereotype irrevocably embedded in the great body of American folklore, it is that of the muscle-bound and moronic campus athlete. He is today and has been for many years the butt of so many jokes that he has become a permanent cliché, like the college widow and the absent-minded professor.

Yet when one puts the myth of the jug-headed, oafish muscle-man under the cold light of logical analysis, it doesn't hold up worth a nickel.

The sophisticates claim the athlete is stupid. Yet in every high school where I've ever worked, the grade-point average of the athletes was above that of the student body as a whole.

The lank-haired leaders of our current literati sneer at the varsity letterman for his juvenile enthusiasms and his willingness to die for dear old Rutgers. But they themselves are quite openly and ardently guilty of enthusiasms over such strange causes as the apotheosis of Joan Baez and the possible canonization of Mario Savio, and they seem ready to die at a moment's notice for a smile from Ho Chi Minh or even for the slightest relaxation of the built-in scowl on Mao Tse-tung. By comparison, dying for Rutgers has its points.

The intellectual vials of wrath are constantly overflowing onto the hapless head of the athlete because of his hopeless Philistinism and his alleged inability to communicate with his peers save in monosyllabic grunts.

Yet the halls of Congress and the board rooms of giant industrial complexes are alike populated by a striking number of ex-athletes who seem to have no difficulty whatever in communicating, and the Philistine mentality of such former contenders on the playing fields as Douglas MacArthur, John F. Kennedy and Justice Byron "Whizzer" White may be left safely for history to judge.

It is presently fashionable to condemn athletic scholarships as anti-intellectual, and to demand that the alumni stop recruiting burly sons of coal miners to advance the colors of old alma mater every Saturday afternoon.

Why?

If an athletic scholarship will permit a youngster who couldn't otherwise afford four years at Random U. to go there, what's wrong with that? And as for coal miners' sons, we don't have enough of them in college anyway.

When such a boy gets his break, of course, he's got to be able to cut the mustard. Once he gets in, he must hit the books and stand or fall on his own ability to study and to master the same subjects as his classmates. If he can't keep up, out he goes.

If I had my way, I would abolish all the hypocritical recruiting restrictions which furnish such regular and sensational fodder for our newspaper sports pages, and I would substitute instead the following very simple rules for athletes in our institutions of higher learning:

(1) Any individual or organization which wants to seek out muscular young men and pay their way through college is welcome to do so.

(2) The muscular young men must pass the same en-

trance exams and meet the same scholastic requirements as their less muscular classmates.

(3) The athlete's course of study must be of comparable status and difficulty with that of the non-athlete.

(4) Nobody gets any special consideration in testing or grading, and flunk-out rules apply to everyone equally.

These four little commandments would do the trick, I think. I have to confess a lifelong fondness for the gridiron gladiators. Over the years, I have seen a remarkable number of them fighting and even dying for their country, and remarkably few of them ending up in jail or taking the Fifth Amendment before a Congressional investigating committee. They seem to be conspicuously absent from Communist-inspired demonstrations and Filthy Speech movements.

Rah! Rah! Rah!

THE ROAD TO FACELESSNESS
Grades are like paychecks. Pretty important . . .

A recent story from one of the great wire services dwelt lightly on the fact that more and more colleges these days are experimenting with "pass-fail" marking systems, trying to escape from "the harmful pressures of letter grades." The theory apparently is that there are only two kinds of students, or human beings, for that matter: those who can manage to cut the mustard and those who can't.

But what about those who not only can cut the mustard, but also can add to it and improve it and make it taste better and last longer and finally come up with a new kind of mustard altogether? Presumably these intellectual virtuosos are now to be submerged in the general ocean of gray-flanneled mediocrity, allowed perhaps to come up once in a while for air—preferably at night—but never, never for recognition. After all, if some of us are to get better grades than others, won't this induce negative feelings of envy and disappointment in the rest of us? And what is an institution of higher learning for, if not to substitute at all costs for these negative feelings the glowingly positive ones of togetherness and ingroupness and ongoing forward-lookingness?

I'll tell you what it's for. It is to encourage and to exhort and if necessary to prod young people into surpassing their own previous best efforts and in the process to inspire them to seek after every ounce of distinction they can manage to win.

Now how in blazes are you going to spur them up and over the hurdles on the race for distinction, Professor, if you have previously and carefully removed not only the trappings of distinction, but also the very distinction itself? Why bother to work up a sweat by racing at all?

The stealthy attempt to ambush A-B-C-D-F grades down in the elementary and junior high schools was unmasked a good many years ago. It was one of Progressive Education's favorite gambits, and the disciples of John Dewey made no bones about their ultimate goal: the abolition of all "artificial" differences among children based upon mere mastery of subject matter. Compared to the bliss of "life adjustment," command of reading, spelling or the multiplication tables were hopelessly inconsequential and trivial. So why go to the trouble of attaching letter grades to "subjects" which really aren't important anyhow?

Besides, parents are apt to attach far too much importance to grades. They're so annoyingly concerned with whether or not Junior knows anything which can be measured objectively. Why can't they forget this nonsense about his grasp of subject matter and concentrate instead upon the really important goal of modern education: Junior's happy, easy, comfortable acceptance by his "peer group"?

I have watched for many years the paving with pious platitudes of this particular descent to Avernus in our public schools. But I really didn't expect to see our colleges falling for the old pitch at this late date, particularly since the high schools and elementary schools are beginning to awaken and stir uneasily as the 30-year spell under which so many of them have slumbered begins to crack.

When the Tartars conquered European Russia during the Middle Ages, they followed the invariable policy of discouraging revolts among their suffering subjects by promptly chopping off any heads which rose above the masses of enslaved Slavs. After several centuries of such lopping and pruning, local political initiative and drive had well-nigh disappeared, leaving the world of Russia passive and quiescent under the knout of the Romanovs and later under the machine-guns and barbed wire of Joe Stalin. Today's traveler home from Muscovy invariably comments upon the surprising lack of dissent within that vast and sprawling domain.

No wonder. A great leader is always a great dissenter, and dissent was bred out of them centuries ago by discouraging their natural leaders, drastically and effectively.

We've found a better way here at home, I guess. After all, you don't have to chop off a leader's head to keep him from seeking fulfillment and eminence. Just amputate any hint of fulfillment and eminence from leadership—and do it at an early age.

Why try to be a leader, anyway? It's so much trouble. Just pass and forget it.

PROPAGANDA IN OUR CLASSROOOMS
Both sides, please. And no fudging . . .

A leading Communist organizer had been invited to address the students of one of my state's large high schools. An obbligato of roars from irate parents mingled with plaintive squeals from the school principal as he dangled over the slow fire of public criticism which he had kindled for himself. As the top school administrator of this state I was invited to take a stand one way or another.

Parenthetically, I might add that "invite" is not precisely the right word here. The invitation came from behind the slitted, steely eyes and the clenched jaws of both parties and resembled nothing so much as a summons from one of Castro's firing squads.

As luck would have it, I was able to take refuge behind a legal prohibition against attempting to advocate or inculcate the principles of communism in public schools, and I honestly believe that as far as elementary and high school children are concerned, this prohibition is both right and proper.

But what about our colleges and universities?

Should Gus Hall, for instance, be given the keys to the campus and permitted to serve up his own peculiar, Communist version of history and economics to a captive audience of teen-age underclassmen?

Should the Imperial Wizard of the Ku Klux Klan be solicited, in the name of free speech, to indoctrinate minors with anthropological and biological "facts" which serious scientists place in the same category as *Grimm's Fairy Tales?*

I think perhaps they should. With one big "IF."

There would be no kick coming from me if Mr. Hall mounted a soap-box right smack in the middle of my own alma mater's quad—IF another soap-box within reasonable hearing distance was occupied by the familiar and formidable figure of J. Edgar Hoover, who would be given the immediate opportunity to bat Hall's lies out of the ball park as fast as he served them over the plate.

And there is no harm whatever in letting the kids listen to the Imperial Wizard likening Negroes to lower animals —IF Roy Wilkins or Ralph Bunche can be on the same platform to give the Wiz a few lessons in the gentle art of debate. I have few questions as to whom the students would place in the "lower" animal category after such a demonstration.

What I object to is giving either the Commies or the Klansmen a free, unhindered, unrebutted crack at the kids on a tax-supported campus. And I do not want the rebuttal to be from some kindly, scholarly, local professor, either. I want it to be from some out-of-towner with the same expertise, gumption and reputation as the original propagandist.

The same thing goes for textbooks. The reason people got hot under the collar a few years ago about using UNESCO material as textbooks was that it is written largely by writers in the employ of the United Nations. They have a vested interest to protect, and such an interest negates automatically the attitude of scholarly pursuit of truth which should be the prerequisite of all textual material.

I have the same objection to using UNESCO writing as textbooks that I would have to using a textbook on the American Revolution written by King George III and his Tory cabinet. It constitutes special pleading by persons with axes to grind.

And I just don't happen to think that public school classrooms are the proper place for either special pleading or ax-grinding.

The College Crisis

In the Fifties, the elementary schools were in trouble.

Today it's the colleges. Because that's where the population bulge of the Fifties is in the Sixties.

By the Seventies, it'll be something else . . .

WANTED: A COLLEGIATE 'MR. CLEAN'
Why bother to have college presidents at all
if they're not going to mind the store?

The capers of a sizable minority of our college students
have caused a good many people to wonder audibly who's
in charge of our institutions of higher learning these days:
the administrators or the students? The wondering isn't
confined to uninformed laymen, either. I am a profesional
school administrator, and I have to admit being pretty
puzzled myself as to who's running the store.

'Twas not always thus. Shortly after the turn of the
century, 250 undergraduates in one of our great universities
went on strike to force the administration to grant them
certain fringe benefits such as beer in the dormitories and
female visitors in their rooms.

The university president promptly expelled all 250 of the
strikers and when the rumor was reported to him that some
of the remaining scholars might stage a mass protest in
favor of the expellees, he announced grimly that he was
prepared to extend the ouster as far as might prove necessary. And that was that.

This kind of simple and direct action would of course

be incomprehensible to our more enlightened college officials today. Most of them are trained and experienced negotiators and moderators, skilled in the subtle techniques of mediation, and dedicated worshipers at the shrine of compromise. They shrink in almost physical revulsion from the merest suggestion that sometimes in dealing with the young, the immature and the cocky it's necessary to lower the boom.

They all seem to be in agreement, positively vying with one another to see who can delegate the most power to the faculty and the student body, establish the largest number of campus "discussion groups" to argue about things and set up the most staff committees to share the blame and to divide the responsibility.

As a result I've just about given up suggesting that our college presidents enforce rules against campus sit-ins, lie-ins, teach-ins or even drink-ins. They tell me that such phenomena are now an inextricable part of the brave new academic world which dawned blushingly upon the national horizon quite recently and which has already fathered such hopeful and promising offshoots as the Aid to the Viet Cong crusade and the Filthy Speech Movement.

But before it is too late I would like to urge that some consideration be given to the enforcement of at least one basic regulation shared by every campus in the country: minimum aesthetic and hygienic standards.

Every news photo and television shot I've seen of the continuing collegiate demonstrations and protest marches features a cast of characters who appear to have taken a common lifelong vow against bathing. After viewing films of the recent Vietnam Day celebrations complete with sound and color, I was impelled to offer a small prayer of thanks that Smell-O-Vision is still in the future.

Surely it is not inconsistent with the First Amendment for a college to require a certain amount of simple cleanliness on the part of its eager majors in civil disobedience and draft-card destruction. As it is now, too many of them look as though their main grievance was against the board of health.

Then there's the problem of campus appearance. Every university I'm familiar with spends umpteen thousands of dollars every year to keep its buildings and grounds looking attractive and tasteful. It doesn't make sense to invest all this money in beauty and then uglify the whole scene with hillbilly beards, beat-up guitars and clothes which look as though they could stand up in a corner all by themselves.

Luckily, a ray of hope is shining on this murky milieu, and it emanates from Washington, of all places. I'm sure no man can solve the problem, but Lady Bird is no man. And she has declared war on the unsightly, praise be.

Could I persuade you to go with me on a campus tour, Mrs. J.?

who's going to run the store?
I'm afraid, Dr. H., that he who pays the piper will continue to call the tune . . .

The erudite Dr. Robert Maynard Hutchins, who has more degrees than a thermometer, recently advocated in his nationally syndicated column that we turn our college campuses over to the professors, get out of their way, and let them mold the leaders of tomorrow.

As I understand Dr. Hutchins, he wants the learned dons to run the campus, select their president and hire and fire each other. The good doctor practically guarantees the millenium in higher education when and if this happy day is ushered in.

May I file a modest dissent?

First off, let me establish my bona fides. I am not—alas —a professor, although I have served a stint of graduate lecturing in one of our largest universities. Nevertheless —to recoin a phrase—some of my best friends are professors, and I have been associating rather intimately with the cap-and-gown set for more than 30 years. I serve on the governing board of the biggest state college system in the land and as a regent of the nation's mightiest university. So I have more than a passing acquaintance with our friend the professor and with his problems.

These, incidentally, he has plenty of. He has to decide pretty quickly whether he is going to remain a seeker after the truth, as he used to be, or to continue to project his current image as a somewhat strident promoter of personal causes and even as a mortarboarded hawker of ideological snake oil.

He needs to take a stand on this asinine "publish or perish" policy, which annually relegates to the academic scrap-heap some of our most brilliant and inspirational teachers just because they have been too busy illuminating students' minds to find time to do a research project on

Etruscan tomb carvings, or to contribute esoteric articles to professional journals which nobody reads.

He desperately needs to find an answer to the increasing challenge posed by the erosion of all personal contact between student and instructor in the great educational factories which our institutions of higher learning are rapidly becoming.

In short, he has his hands full in his own proper bailiwick, too full to start looking around for other problems to grab onto, Dr. Hutchins to the contrary notwithstanding.

American universities are not European universities. Over here we cling to the perhaps quaint idea that the people's institutions ought to be run by the people who support and populate them, not by employees who are hired to do certain things inside them. It is true that in Europe and in South America, universities are run by their inmates, and have been for a long time. This is one thing which makes us different from Europe and South America. And *vive la différence*!

A professor is a trained and dedicated expert, true enough. He has every right to enjoy academic freedom and tenure and the priceless boon of free inquiry into the ultimate nature of truth. But he has no right at all to take over and operate the tax-supported state universities and colleges of this country, any more than the janitors or groundskeepers or secretaries who also work within the ivied walls of Academe have such a right.

It has been rightly said—and I'm sure Dr. Hutchins would agree—that the ultimate reality of all education is the impact of the personality of the instructor upon the mind of the student. But there is nothing in this concept which implies even remotely that either the instructor or the student should be setting or administering the underlying policy of the institution wherein he lives and works.

In a democracy, all the people have the right to determine policy in their own institutions. And a public university, whether Dr. Hutchins likes the idea or not, is still a democratic institution.

THE WORRIED GENERATION
College students have no monopoly on anxiety.
If it falls, the bomb will fall on all of us . . .

Puncturing myths is a thankless task at best, but there are times when it must be done. Currently, the number-one figure of our national imagination is the distraught, neurotic teen-ager, hagridden with fears of imminent nuclear annihilation and saddled with a world of insoluble puzzles which he has inherited from us.

Oh, come now. It has always been thus.

College boys in midnight bull sessions, it is said, frighten themselves with horror stories of the hell-bomb sterilizing the planet. In my day, my brothers in deal old Sigma Pi were trying to figure out just where we could go to escape the appalling poison-gas war which was just around the corner. Everybody from H. G. Wells to Robert W. Chambers was rushing into print with portrayals of the diabolic effect upon the human race of Lewisite and "Green-Cross" gas, which all the major powers possessed in abundance and were certain to unleash at the merest rattle of a saber.

This was in the Hungry Thirties, and we depression dwellers divided our worry time equally between the unspeakable nature of gas warfare and the unemployable nature of ourselves. The latter concern was our second great bugaboo. With very little effort even the most diligent collegiate candidate for Phi Beta Kappa could conjure up a bone-chilling vision of himself selling apples on a blizzardy street corner—and with a certain amount of obvious justification.

Despite our youthful alarums and excursions into these and other apocalyptic byways, however, we survived. At least the overwhelming majority of us did. Some of us were indeed killed in a war, just as some in every generation of man since time began have been killed, but we were not all gassed to death.

And this despite the fact that every nation in those days did indeed have huge stockpiles of the stuff cached away, and a madman named Hitler might certainly have been expected to use it when Germany started to go down the drain in 1945.

Similarly, the bull-session boys were wrong about their careers as potential anchor men on the bread line. Shortly after my generation got out of college, the nation embarked upon the most fabulous period of business prosperity in the history of the world, and most of my fearful fraternity brothers are much lusher and plusher today than their fathers ever thought of being.

Who in the mid-Thirties would have dreamed of World War II without poison gas? Yet, that's the way it turned out.

Who in the depth of the Depression could have possibly

envisioned the gross national product, the miraculous standard of living and the 95% employment of today? But that's
the way the dice came up.

So you'll pardon me when I turn a somewhat jaundiced
eye upon some of the more highly publicized whiners and
whimperers who purport to speak for the beards-and-
Benzedrine set these days.

If they elect to wallow in their pads in a permanent orgy
of self-pity and to drape themselves over the fences of
military installations, where cleaner and guttier youngsters
are learning how to defend all of us, and to tear up their
draft cards as a final gesture of surrender, then let them
blame it on their own lack of heart and sense, not on the
possibility of the H-bomb.

And if they elect to follow permanent careers as demonstrators, rioters and sit-downers instead of going out and
getting paying jobs, let them hold their own sloth and
slovenliness responsible, not the minuscule 5% unemploy-
ment rate which would have seemed heaven right here on
earth to my classmates and me.

I know, man. It's this world. Like, it bugs you.

Well, a little DDT might help. But like charity, let it
begin at home. Right in that old pad.

'PUBLISH OR PERISH': IDIOCY IN A MORTARBOARD
*In memory of the countless undergraduate hours
I spent being bored stiff by dithering dons . . .*

Turn with me to page 77 in the 1966 yearbook of dear old
Random University. There, among the blandly benign faces

of the faculty, you will find Asst. Prof. Bacca and Assoc. Prof. Laureate, both of whom teach history and one of whom is about to get fired.

Dr. Bacca is scrawny, rumpled and distracted. He is the recent author of such fascinating research studies as "The Role of Dandruff in the Career of Aaron Burr" and "The Micturition Patterns of Bismarck's Doberman Pinschers," both of which were published in the *International Journal of Professional Puerility*. His voice is inaudible past the first row of his classroom, but this is of no consequence for two reasons:

1—His lectures are so incredibly bad that he even bores himself on the infrequent occasions when he is called upon to deliver one; and

2—He's currently on top-secret special assignment with the CIA, writing an historical analysis of economic trends in Southeast Asia dating from the reign of Emperor Hoo Hee in 1263 B.C. This little gem, duly translated into North Vietnamese and enclosed in Chinese fortune cookies, will be dropped on Hanoi in the hope that it will bore the Viet Cong to death. Meanwhile, the good professor hasn't seen a college student to talk to for an academic coon's age.

Dr. Laureate, on the other hand, teaches three classes a day. He's tall, tweedy and titillating. He brings the dead past to life with a bang which makes his lectures far and away the most popular in all of Random U. Since he joined the faculty three years ago he has interested more undergraduates in history than have all the other members of the department put together, which in itself would not be saying a heck of a lot. But he's sparkling. He's humorous. He's interesting.

Postscript: He has never written anything for publication.

Now you tell me which of the two is getting the well-known can tied to him, and if you say "Prof. Bacca," you are out of your mind.

Almost every university in the country compels its instructors to meet a certain rigid quota of professional writing and recondite research if they want to stay on the job. It doesn't matter if the prof hates to write or if he is a lousy researcher but a brilliant lecturer.

"Publish or Perish" is the prevailing motto, and a squirrel-headed, idiotic one it is, too.

One of the most scholarly research profs I ever knew was such a crummy lecturer that he invariably sidled into class laden with about 14 ponderous tomes dealing with his specialty and then for the next hour regaled his desperate audience with droning excerpts from his dogeared reference volumes.

On the other hand, the finest instructor I had as an undergraduate was an expatriate Russian prince who had escaped from his native land in 1917 one jump ahead of the Bolsheviks and who had never written a research paper in his life. Yet when he lectured on European history in his broken English he set the class on fire with interest and enthusiasm.

The theory behind "Publish or Perish" is, of course, the deliriously double-barreled nonsequitur that:

1—The purpose of a university is to conduct research, and

2—Therefore, a professor should add further accretions of published research to his institution's already heavily encrusted image.

I deny both theses.

The reason an institution of higher learning is supported by the public is that it may instruct the public's sons and daughters. Once this truism is accepted, it follows that the main duty of a professor is to teach young people.

I happen to believe that there is an important place for both instruction and research on any campus. But I see no earthly reason to assume that both functions have to be performed by every professor. Let the researcher research. Let the lecturer lecture.

A professor has enough problems these days. Let's not compel him in addition to function as an intellectual hermaphrodite.

A HERETICAL LOOK AT THE DRAFT
On the theory that everybody ought to get
into the act . . .

Why aren't the draft-card burners being drafted themselves?

Why don't we give the male hippies a shave, a shower and a fast ship to Vietnam?

Why aren't the Hell's Angels in uniform instead of in black leather jackets?

In short, why can't we give the bums, the creeps and the delinquents the job of chivying Ho Chi Minh and his merry murderers around the swamps and jungles of Southeast Asia instead of killing off the cream of our decent young manhood in this nightmare in which our country is currently participating?

I'll tell you why we can't.

Because our armed forces just plain don't want them.

Because these misfits in open-toed sandals would be just as big misfits in Army boots.

And finally because ever since Agamemnon's warriors debouched upon the ringing plains of windy Troy, and no doubt long before that, a nation has always found it necessary to send its best men—not its worst—to any war it wanted to win.

The current uproar over draft deferments is nothing new. I well remember the "total mobilization" of World War II and the problem with the zoot-suiters and pachucos of those dim, dead days. World War I had its slackers and its lounge-lizards. A Civil War reluctant dragon could fork over a few hundred greenbacks and pay a substitute to do his fighting for him. And I presume that Julius Caesar and Alexander the Great had similar headaches.

The problem, then, is not new. I am disturbed, however, over the educational deferments recently under congressional attack. During the early Forties everybody was subject to the draft except key workers in science and defense industries. An "A" college student usually stayed in school, all right, but he was in uniform and under military orders.

Today the apparent policy is to defer college students who maintain a high grade-point average and let them keep their civilian status. I can't see this for several reasons.

For one thing, it puts a completely unfair burden upon the colleges themselves. It's hard enough at best to give a grade, if only because every instructor knows that a student's academic standing and indeed his whole future career may hinge upon the grade he gets in a key subject. But when you tell that instructor that not only the student's possible livelihood, but also his life itself may hang upon that little mark upon a card, I submit that you introduce such a traumatic element into the teacher-student relationship as to vitiate and disrupt the whole instructional setup.

In addition, there is the whole question of just how universal our selective service ought to be. The theory is that a young man who achieves highly in school is in effect serving his country by qualifying himself for future leadership in science, technology or statesmanship.

So be it. But is there any good reason why an able-bodied young scholar shouldn't have his service potential dignified by his country in the form of induction into its armed forces and subsequent assignment to a hitch in an appropriate institution of higher learning?

The principle behind selective service is precisely what the name implies. It's that of selectivity: a place for everybody, and everybody in his place. End result in view: the equitable utilization of our available manpower to insure the survival of our country.

In the light of this principle properly understood, and in the face of the undeniable fact that we are presently at war, two things at least should be crystal clear:

1—A young hood may belong in jail; he doesn't belong in the Army.

2—A young scholar certainly belongs in college; he should in a time of national crisis attend it in the service of his country.

HOW FREE IS FREE SPEECH?
There's a limit to everything. Even the
inalienable right to make a public jackass
out of oneself . . .

I regret to report a serious epidemic currently raging within
a segment of our American college population. The disease
is an ancient one called logorrhea, and it is characterized
by one invariable symptom: a severe and uncontrolled running off at the mouth.

In the good old days, logorrhea was endemic rather than
epidemic, confined to such individual plague centers as
local bridge clubs, Eugene O'Neill plays and the halls of
Congress. But of late it has become virulently contagious,
spreading out all over the map, especially in our institutions
of higher learning.

What concerns me is its recent tendency to seek out and
infect the emotionally and mentally immature and to masquerade under such alluring false colors as constitutional
rights and foreign policy dialogues.

It is no accident that the modern trend toward complete
campus anarchy has labeled itself the Free Speech Movement. Like Shakespeare's "divinity which hedges a king,"
there is apparently such big medicine clinging to the phrase
"free speech" that the Savios and the Apthekers invariably
use it as an opening gambit in their never-ending game to
destroy higher education in this country.

No society has ever tolerated unbridled license disguised
as free speech, if only because society would come apart
at the seams if it did any such thing. There are all kinds of

restrictions on our right to sound off. There always have been.

For instance, I can't urge someone to dismember you with a carving knife. You can't accuse me of wife-beating, either—unless, of course, you can prove it. And Justice Holmes' acid comment upon the "right" of some joker to yell "Fire!" in a crowded theater is too well-known to warrant repeating here. No one can use the Constitution to advance the cause of riot, obscenity or treason.

Our college students ought to be old enough to understand this. They ought to be able to understand something else, too: that the purpose of an institution of higher learning is not to afford them a built-in public address system and a captive audience.

The purpose is to make them learned. It is to teach them to pursue the truth and to recognize it when and if they catch up with it. It is to hand from one generation to the next the intellectual artifacts which are the rungs of the great ladder leading us over the centuries from savagery to civilization.

Students are in school to learn, not to instruct—to listen, not to shoot their mouths off. When they have become at least partially educated, they may be worth listening to by the rest of us. Until that time, quite frankly, they are not. If they were already well-grounded in the cultural heritage of the race and in the ability to think in an orderly and disciplined fashion, there would be no need for them to be in college.

A court of justice does not permit unlimited free speech within its halls. Try it and see how quickly you land in contempt of court. Congress does not allow spectators in the gallery to harangue it under cover of the Third Amendment. No church in its right ecclesiastical mind will let some nut in the congregation stand up in the middle of Sunday services and bellow random blasphemies.

Why should a college or university be any different?

In public institutions, we address our peers in accordance with rules previously set up through democratic processes. We do not unilaterally insist upon imposing our own whims and crotchets upon others and then shouting "free speech!" when some of those others object to having to listen to us.

The Berkeley demonstrations and the illegitimate progeny which they have spawned across the land all stem from the refusal of the demonstrators to recognize one abiding truth: that in a democratic society, the small minority does not try to impose its will upon the great majority by force.

In a totalitarian state, such goings-on are par for the course.

Who knows? Maybe this is what the "new activists" are trying to get us conditioned to.

GETTING BAGGED IN CLASS MAY BE A GOOD IDEA
*Getting bagged in my day meant something
a little different . . .*

A titillating tidbit of trivia was wafted to us last year out of the great Northwest, where one of the college professors, acting in the scholarly and dignified tradition of his great calling, announced that he had enrolled a bag in one of his classes. I'm glad to note that the good doctor hastened to add that it was a real bag, and a black bag to boot. There

it sat in the professor's class, all zippered up tight, as anony-
mously uncommunicative as a fireplug. Presumptively it
was occupied, for every now and then a sepulchrally
muffled voice issued from its baggy depths, attesting not
only to the humanity, but also to the hardihood of its
oxygen-starved inmate.

It is reliably reported that no one knows who occupied
the bag. The professor claimed the whole thing was an experiment, designed to test the reactions of students to the
presence of a faceless, armless, legless Thing in their midst
as a continuing fact of what he is pleased to call their
academic life. The spectrum of dutifully reported student
responses, naturally enough, ran the predictable gamut
from rapport to ribaldry.

I suppose this kind of experiment is after all superior to
the usual tired old collegiate inquiries into knee-jerk re-
flexes and panty-raid syndromes, but I wonder if there
might not be more profound nuances to Project Bag than
a mere superficial scrutiny of sophomore behavior patterns.

For instance, the professor might try bagging himself
instead of the student. In my dim and distant undergraduate
days I had several profs who would have been immeasur-
ably improved by the addition of several layers of good
thick gunnysacking.

One of them wiggled his ears distractingly when excited,
and another waggled his Phi Beta Kappa key when afflicted
with ennui. And I guess it's true that every little movement
has a meaning all its own, because I can't seem to remember
much about either the instructors or their subjects except
the rhythmic peculiarities of their respective muscular contortions.

I am prepared to say, however, that neither health nor safety would have been inhibitory factors in such an experiment, since both of these worthy dons could easily have bored their way out of anything, including a bag, given a few minutes to warm up.

Student demonstrators, too, might consider a pouch as an aid to the pursuit of pacifism. Think of the moral effect of hundreds of silent duffel bags, each projecting a placard and sporting an artificial beard, sitting dumpily and morosely outside the local draft headquarters, mute protests to the indignity of being asked to serve one's country.

And the concept of bagging Hubert Horatio Humphrey instead of booing him when he conducts one of his sporadic campus safaris conjures up a vision which I prefer at the moment to hug silently to my bosom and which may even open up hitherto undreamed-of dimensions to the job of being Vice President.

Seriously, I'll tell you why this bag business may catch on and spread. It signifies the first attempt of the student to isolate himself from the professor, whereas for the past several years it has been the other way around. The full professor, at least since Sputnik and the advent of unprecedented federal largesse in the form of academic projects and grants-in-aid, has been increasingly attempting to isolate himself from his students. In many of our larger institutions of higher learning, the more prestigious Nobel Prize-winning profs never meet with an undergraduate class from one year to the next. The real work of the university is more and more being done by young, willing, but callow teaching assistants.

Maybe it's about time the collegians gave the professors

a taste of their own medicine. Going around in bags might put across the idea, and in some selected cases might even improve the general aesthetic appearance of the campus.

Except that bagging will probably prove ineffective when applied to a few of the more case-hardened activists who currently infest the groves of Academe. In which case it may not be completely out of line to recommend sacking them.

Education in Depth

Anybody who thinks Progressive Education is dead had better think again.

The Gospel According to St. John Dewey is still very much with us.

But within the past six years, a new philosophy has elbowed its way into the educational arena.

The fight is now on. To the finish.

THE FIVE MAIN PURPOSES OF EDUCATION
*If every school would teach to these ends, we'd
still have lots of problems in education. But
they wouldn't be problems of what
to teach ...*

An old, old story is told of a certain philosopher who in a
dream one night was visited by Minerva, goddess of wisdom.
In partial repayment for a long life of dedication to philosophy, she offered him the answer to one question, with no
strings attached.

"Tell me, O goddess," cagily quoth the sage, "how I may
find the one unfailing path to truth, justice and virtue?"

"That's easy," quipped his Olympian visitant briskly.
"Just define your terms."

And with that she vanished in a flurry of ectoplasm, after
the annoying manner of goddesses.

I was reminded of old Min the other day when I received
this letter from one of my less ecstatic correspondents.

"You're always talking about the strengths, weaknesses
and problems of education. I notice, however, that you
never quite get around to defining your terms. What is

education or, rather, what should it be? What's the purpose of education anyway?"

It doesn't have one, sir. It has five, and here they are.

1—*To pursue the truth.*

Yes, sir. The truth. No matter where it may be or how cleverly it may be concealed. It is a never-ending chase, of course, and being mortal, erring humans, we may never quite catch up with truth and hold it cupped in our hands. The very search for it, though, cannot but ennoble those who spend their lives in such a quest.

2—*To hand down the cultural heritage of the race.*

Otherwise each generation would have to spend its valuable time reinventing the wheel. Or writing "Hamlet." Or splitting the atom. Education focuses the accumulated wisdom of the past upon the vexing problems of the present in order to make possible a better future. Or at least it should.

3—*To teach organized, disciplined, systematic subject matter.*

Not life adjustment, togetherness, in-groupness or happy, easy, comfortable acceptance by one's peer group. The only thing which enables man to dominate a savagely hostile environment is knowledge of specific subject matter and the ability to use it as a means of keeping said environment tamed and in its place. This old saw is especially pertinent for present-day America, whose planetary environment is currently so downright hostile as to be positively hair-raising.

4—To help the individual realize his own potential.

Until relatively recently, concern with the individual was the be-all and the end-all of my profession. Of late we've been plunging up all kinds of blind alleys labeled "group counseling," "group psychological testing" and an educators' version of "group therapy." We'd better get the individual back into the educational spotlight unless, of course, we want to opt for the ant-hill, mass-Pavlovian-reflex training which the Russians have substituted for real education. The latter is cheaper, and more efficient. It just isn't education.

5—To ensure the survival of our country.

If Uncle Sam goes down the drain, so does our whole educational establishment with its practitioners. Something else would take its place, no doubt, but it would be pretty unrecognizable, except perhaps to somebody like George Orwell. In fact, we educators had better do whatever is necessary to see that Uncle Sam stays around a while longer. Unless we're ready to change our vocation, that is.

There. I've defined my terms. For my money, these are the five purposes of education.

You will notice that none of them has much to do with adjustment to environment or with the achievement of popularity within one's group or even with making a fast buck. These things can be taught, all right, but the process is not real education.

Sorry about that.

NEEDED: A CRUSADE AGAINST SLOPPY EDUCATIONAL THINKING
*Education has too many Neville Chamberlains,
umbrellas and all. Schools exist not to
compromise with wrong, but to
uphold the right . . .*

How about helping me hamburgerize a few sacred cows?

Two of the bovines in question are off-the-cuff remarks credited to two of our most esteemed and even beloved Americans: Will Rogers and Father Flanagan of Boys' Town.

The immortal Will was supposed to have quipped in a moment of euphoria: "I never met a man I didn't like." And the good padre presumably voiced the classic comment: "There is no such thing as a bad boy."

Now just a darned minute, as Lonesome George used to say.

If Will Rogers had lived a sheltered, cloistered life—say in a Trappist monastery—I might buy his universal admiration for *genus homo*. But the great rope-and-repartee artist led a checkered and highly gregarious existence and rubbed elbows with thousands of people, including some of the biggest heels of all time.

Surely Will didn't like the Pretty Boy Floyd and Al Capone-types who used to hang around backstage at the Follies while he was starring for Ziegfeld. Equally certainly he couldn't have enjoyed a social evening with Leopold and Loeb, the thrill killers of the Twenties. And if wise, kindly Rogers had ever met Hitler or Stalin, I'm sure he would have disliked those sinister and bloody paranoiacs profoundly.

Verily the Rogers tongue must have been firmly lodged in the Rogers cheek when he kidded that he'd never met anybody he disliked.

The Flanagan dictum about the nonexistent bad boy, however, was deadly serious and strikes close to home. During a lifetime in education I have worked with almost as many boys as good old Mr. Chips—all sizes, shapes, colors and dispositions—and unfortunately some of them were bad.

Definitions, of course, are important. If to Father Flanagan the word "bad" meant totally vile, mortally depraved or eternally damned, then I'm with him. I've never known a bad boy, either. But if we are to attach less extreme meanings to the little adjective, then you're darned right there are such things as bad boys—plenty of them.

What I'm leading up to is an indictment of still a third sacred cow, this time a more recent example of educational self-kidding. An official of the National Education Association was musing the other day over the increasingly desperate problem of classroom discipline and downright mayhem. Dr. Charles Bish delivered himself of the following little gem:

"We don't know how to teach in culture-conflict areas, and we need to learn fast. Teachers flee not because the kids use swear words, but because they don't feel at home in the area.

"I asked one boy if he was learning. He said, 'Yeah. She's a good teacher. She just gets shook at a little fighting.'

"We have to adjust to others' attitudes, and quickly."

There speaks the true progressive educationist. Adjust to your environment at any cost. Don't try to change things. After all, nothing is really "right" or "wrong."

Bunk.

What's wrong with teaching the kid that fighting in school is wrong?

Why not outlaw profanity and bring back the good old soap-in-the-mouth bit for youngsters who can't keep a clean tongue in their heads? The school exists to make Johnny a better boy, not to kid him into thinking it's okay to talk like the late Lennie Bruce. And if a school can't hold up to its pupils a vision of higher standards, proper conduct and purer speech, what good is it?

I don't want the teacher to get used to Johnny's fighting and swearing. I want the teacher to make Johnny cut it out.

And rather than teach the teacher to feel comfortably at home in the slum, I want him to know that it *is* a slum and be inspired with a burning itch to change it and then to communicate this itch to his pupils.

We Americans have never been noted either for running away from a crummy environment or for adjusting to it.

In the past, we took our environment and shook it up and hammered it and reshaped it closer to our heart's desire.

What's wrong with that as a recipe for tomorrow, too?

THE MULTISENSORY APPROACH
*A horrible example of what I've been complaining
about for a quarter of a century . . .*

To one who has been crusading for some years against the
greatest evil ever to be inflicted upon education, it is vastly
discouraging to get letters like this:

"Dear Sir: Why do you keep harping about progressive
education? My education professor at Blank University tells
me that progressive education went out of the schools more
than 10 years ago."

It is certainly true that the life-adjustment boys began
to soft-pedal the term "progressive education" during the
mid-Fifties. Unfortunately, the name had developed a
rather poor public image, and it became necessary to
camouflage it under various and sundry aliases. But to
assume that a thing is dead merely because it changes its
name is as stupid as the Missouri sheriffs would have been
a century ago had they stopped looking for Jesse James
simply because he started calling himself Mr. Howard.

For all you gentle readers who believe everything your
professors tell you, then, let me share with you a recent
letter from one of my old, fellow school-principals whom
we shall call Bill:

"A bunch of us went over to the annual school institute
and found ourselves scheduled to visit a third-grade class
which everyone said was an educational wonder. It certainly was.

"When we went into the room we found it tastefully
decorated with Japanese mobiles and hand-painted lanterns.

Individual woven mats were on the floor, and the kids were all dressed up in authentic Japanese costumes, obviously handmade by Mother at the cost of considerable time and effort."

My friend's curiosity was sufficiently aroused to ask the demonstration teacher what was going on.

"Oh," she said brightly, "we are concluding a unit on silk, and we are using the multisensory approach."

"What," asked Bill diffidently, "might be the multi-sensory approach to silk?"

It turned out to be really something. Children, it seems, can't really get to know silk just by reading about it. On Monday the class had been subjected to the visual approach and had viewed slides and films of silk in its various meta-morphoses.

Tuesday had been set aside for the auditory approach, with the pupils listening to tape recordings of typical sounds in a Japanese silk factory. Then on Wednesday the tactile approach to the subject had been unleashed, and the kids had handled samples of silken commodities passed around the room for them to feel at will.

"Unfortunately," the teacher sighed regretfully, "silk has no taste or smell, so we will have to forego those approaches."

My friend was impressed.

"What happens today?" he inquired.

"The climax of the silk unit," replied the instructor happily. "Today the children utilize the 'large-muscle' approach to silk."

And at her signal all the small fry got down on their

mats, kimonos and all, and for 10 minutes of "free activity" imitated the gyrations and contortions of the silkworms as they spin their cocoons, or whatever it is that silkworms spin.

"At that," my friend concluded in his letter, "I went out into the corridor, looked about to see if I was alone and then quietly beat my head against the wall."

I felt for him, of course, but I wrote back and told him he must have been hallucinating. After all, progressive education is dead. The professors say so, and so, of course, he couldn't have been seeing and hearing what he thought he was.

One thought did occur to me, though. By a conservative estimate, there must be about five million substances other than silk. I'd like to know how that teacher plans to find enough time to take the "multisensory" approach to all of them.

RELATIVISM IS EDUCATION'S MORTAL ENEMY
*A kind of relative way of thinking which
has absolutely nothing to do with
Einstein . . .*

'Tis the season to be public-opinion polley, so let's try the latest Rafferty Poll on you. How many of you would subscribe to the following way-out statements?

1—If enough kids in a given school class say "I ain't got no book," kindly Miss Mentor should wince momentarily, forget it and concentrate on something more important, like togetherness and on-going forward-lookingness.

2—Children should be given things to read in school that they enjoy rapport with and which have "immediacy" for them, like *Lolita* and *Love-Life of the Beatles,* not compelled to read out-of-date, corny stuff like the *Odyssey* and *Robinson Crusoe.*

3—Students should be encouraged to demonstrate publicly for their particular point of view and to conduct their politics in the streets, even if they haven't been in school long enough to accumulate enough facts to bulwark either their viewpoints or their politics.

Now wait a minute. Before you start another barrage of "Dear-Sir-you-cur" protests rolling in my direction, let me hastily establish my nonauthorship of the aforementioned sentiments. They were authored in considerably more detail than my capsule versions by, respectively:

1—An official of the U.S. Department of Health, Education and Welfare,

2—Bel Kaufman, teacher-author of "Up the Down Staircase,"

3—Frank Mankiewicz, press assistant to Bobby Kennedy.

These are all estimable people and no doubt have profound and even highly ingenious justifications for their seemingly weird points of view. Just the same, there is a rapidly growing snowball of this kind of guff presently rolling down the educational hill toward the little red schoolhouse snuggled in the valley. And the name of that snowball is "relativism."

Webster defines it as "the view that ethical truths depend upon the individuals or groups holding them."

Educationally applied, this means that it's okay for the

school kids to say "ain't" or indeed anything else just so long as everybody's doing it.

Similarly, the term "literary classic" is meaningless because the only thing worth reading is what's cool with the current "in" group.

And how is a teen-ager going to learn civics and current events unless he's out with the Molotov-cocktail set clobbering some cop?

What relativism really implies is the assassination of all absolutes, the strangling of all standards, the vanquishing af all values—except, of course, relative ones. So if Johnny uses hair-raising English, don't substitute the teacher's "middle-middle class" speech patterns for Johnny's "middle-lower class" habits. After all, how can we be sure teacher is right? Can't Johnny be just as right?

No, friends; Johnny can't. English operates under set rules which have little or nothing to do with social stratification or whether Johnny lives on Park Ave. or under a bridge somewhere. In the semantic battle between 'Enry 'Iggins and Eliza Doolittle, Prof. Higgins was right. Obviously.

So spare me the anguished protests that Johnny needs to learn more important things, that English grammar is really Latinized syntax and that it doesn't matter just so Johnny can make himself understood.

It matters a lot. Correct English has to be taught to the next generation unless we want a replay of the Tower of Babel around 1984. And it *does* matter profoundly if Johnny is being encouraged in school to express himself in the latest disk jockeyese instead of in the best of an admittedly evolving Queen's English.

The same thing goes for great literature instead of comic-book drivel and for disciplined, dedicated study instead of downbeat demonstrating.

Every civilization since time began has had certain positive standards and lasting values. Ours is no exception. And the schools exist to uphold and to transmit these values.

Else why have schools at all? Any illiterate savage can practice relativism, and does.

After all, cannibalism is relatively ethical for the cannibal, even if it is relatively uncomfortable for the missionary.

Financing the Schools

Nobody likes to pay school taxes.

As education gets more and more expensive, more and more people are going to be vitally interested in it.

This can't help but be a good thing.

HOW TO SAVE MONEY ON LOCAL SCHOOLS

It's funny how worked up people get over money for schools. How come they don't seem to get emotional over money for sewers?

This is for those of you who are afflicted with the Nyet Syndrome when it comes to education's rapidly increasing costs. First, a few gentle questions:

Are school taxes bleeding you? Do you wince, cringe and rattle like a shocked sidewinder every time your local board of education calls a special revenue election? Are you reading up on how to organize a taxpayers' strike?

Cool it, fellow sufferers. There are lots of ways to make education less expensive, or at least more economical. And without putting Tommy and Susan in tents, either. Here are some practical suggestions, if you'd like to pass them on to your favorite school board member, who incidentally and probably won't appreciate your helpfulness quite as much as you think he ought to. Alas.

1—Plan far, far ahead. At least two decades. Latch onto your future school sites 20 years before they're going to be needed. You'll be surprised how little the land will cost you now, comparatively speaking, and how greedily it will gulp down the tax dollars later on. And don't say your crystal ball is clouded. It will work if you look into it long and prayerfully.

2—When you plan a school building, give it an arbitrary maximum life expectancy of 30 years and build it accordingly. By 1997, educational techniques will have changed so greatly that any school built in 1967 will be as out of date as a Stutz Bearcat.

To show you what happens when school board members insist upon building expensive monuments to themselves for their grandchildren to marvel at, instead of putting up relatively inexpensive educational workshops for one generation of children, let me tell you that I've personally visited midwestern schools erected out of blocks of living granite during the administration of the late U.S. Grant and still full of children today.

Holy Rameses! They might just as well send the kids to school in Grant's Tomb.

3—Automate record keeping, attendance accounting, payroll compiling and over-all business procedures in your local school office. It will cost you temporarily in new equipment, but it will save you so much money in salaries that you will be able to afford all sorts of important things you'd like to buy now but can't. Maybe solid gold goal posts for the new football stadium. Or even a new Cadillac for the winning coach, if it comes to that.

4—Appoint citizens' committees to work with your school board in riding herd on fiscal needs and writing up the guidelines for bond and tax elections. Include a few starry-eyed idealists to think big and an equal number of Ebenezer Scrooges to act as watchdogs of the treasury. Strangely enough, it works. You'll get good schools at bargain prices.

5—Don't insist, Mom, upon huge dinosaurish busses rolling up quietly and expensively to your very doorstep twice every day to pick up and deliver Junior like a freckle-faced carton of Grade A milk. Some busing is necessary these days, what with traffic hazards and all. But busing just to spare Junior a three- or four-block walk along a peaceful neighborhood street to a central pickup point is not only unnecessary, but costly as all get-out. And an active roadblock in the path of the President's physical fitness program, besides.

6—Put merit pay into your schools so your finest, most inspirational teachers will be paid extra. You won't spend less money this way, but you'll certainly get your money's worth for what you do spend.

Yes, there are lots of ways to cut school spending. The trouble is that so many folks—school people as well as terrified taxpayers—tend to get emotionally carried away when a school revenue election goes down the drain. They are apt then to start giving the ax to such things as kindergartens, counseling services and even athletics competition.

Part of the time this is due to sheer panic and honest ignorance.

But a lot of the time it's due to a kind of childish "nyaah-nyaah" desire to get even with those hard-headed "no" voters. We'll show 'em, by golly! We'll cut where it hurts.

It's not the voters you get even with this way. Unfortunately.

It's the kids.

LOCAL CONTROL SHOULD NOT MEAN REPRISALS
*Revenge is a theme for Shakespeare. It's pretty
inappropriate when applied to kids . . .*

Once upon a time there was a small but promising boy who
was the apple of his fond parents' eye. All their future
hopes and happiness were bound up in his restless, wriggling
person. But they were strict and upright people, upholding
standards of decency and seemliness to which they expected
their son to adhere as a matter of course. So when he came
home one day after having fallen from his state of childish
grace, they were appalled.

He had obviously taken up with bad companions. His
clothes were dirty. He had acquired within the hour a
roving and slightly blackened eye. His table talk that evening was unaccountably laced with minced oaths. Worst
of all, he had come down with a bad case of pediculosis;
in short, he was lousy.

So his parents sent him to his room, locked him in and
let him starve to death.

Ridiculous? Of course.

Too ridiculous ever to happen? Not quite.

Oh, it may not happen to an individual child these days.
But it darned well happens to entire school districts which
may be charged with the responsibility of educating thou-

sands and even tens of thousands of individual children. Your children. And it happens quite often because you get sore at one of the teachers or become outraged at the school board for making an even bigger jackass than usual out of itself, and so you get even by voting against the latest school bond issue designed to keep a roof over your own kid's head while he's trying to learn something.

Here's an excerpt out of a particularly dunderheaded letter I got the other day:

"I strongly disapprove of the way our school superintendent conducts himself, and I disapprove even more strongly of his educational philosophy. I've asked our board of education to get rid of him, and they won't do a thing. Now they've got the nerve to ask us to vote them $4 million to build a new high school. I'm organizing my neighborhood to vote against the bond issue. Maybe then the school board will listen to us."

In other words, we're going to get rid of an alleged louse by starving its host.

As our president is fond of saying, "Let's reason together." The new high school is not going to do the superintendent any good, nor the school board either, for that matter. It's presumably intended to give your children and your neighbors' children a place to congregate in, sit down and learn something.

The kind of educational philosophy to which they are going to be exposed while they are sittting there has absolutely nothing to do with the logistics involved in housing our rapidly mushrooming pupil population. Whether it's Progressive Education according to John Dewey or Education in Depth according to Max Rafferty, there has to be a place to teach it which is at least comparatively sheltered from the wind and the rain.

It's equally harum-scarum to vote against school revenue measures because you think the system is insufficiently integrated or too integrated or what have you. Assume you manage at some future date to argue your school board into going for your point of view. If you're going to busy yourself in the meantime turning down worthwhile proposals to construct needed buildings, you'll find yourself practicing your own particular brand of segregation or integration in a vacant lot, and much good may it do you —or your children.

Finally, there are quite a few of us who have seemingly given up on all hopes of controlling the Frankenstein monster of federal expenditure and as a result are lowering the boom on all local school needs, glowering self-righteously the while.

"We may not be able to hog-tie Lyndon," we tell ourselves, "but we can darned sure hog-tie our own school board." And down goes another bond election.

My old home town of Los Angeles is a good example of how this sort of short-sightedness can wreak havoc. Regardless of whether its school philosophy is right or whether it's integrated enough or whether Congress is behaving like a drunken sailor in Washington, there's a city that needs more schools if any city ever did. Yet its last few bond elections have been soundly trounced.

If you don't like what your school board is doing, vote in a new one.

If you don't like the integration pattern, elect people who will work toward the kind you do like.

If you think Congress spends like a prodigal, vote for a few Scrooges in the next national election.

But don't vote down a proposal to build more local schools unless the proposal itself makes no sense. The patient is skinny enough these days. He can be punished in better ways than by being sent to bed without his supper.

EDUCATIONAL NEGLECT EQUALS
NATIONAL INGRATITUDE
*I wonder. Can it be that the longer people
stay in school the more they hate education?*

> *"Education certainly gives victory, although victory
> sometimes produces forgetfulness of education."*

PLATO

This paradox comes to you piping hot from the oven of a recent school bond election in one of our most populous cities. The purpose of said election, incidentally was not to raise teachers' salaries, send the board of education to Squaw Valley, or buy the superintendent a Cadillac. It was to build more schools for the children. Period.

Anyway, it seems that a study was made of the election results, with each precinct classified in accordance with the educational level of its average voter. Thus, those with a preponderance of college graduates were labeled "high," those whose residents had gone through high school were "medium," and the ones whose citizenry had mostly dropped out of school before getting past the tenth grade were, naturally enough, "low."

Then the educational level of each precinct was compared with its support or nonsupport of the school bonds. The results were fascinating.

The sharp-honed, well-trained brains of the "high" neighborhoods turned out en masse to vote "no" on the proposal to build badly needed schools for the kids. In fact, if it had been left to the college alumni, their fellow townsmen's children could have sat out in the wind and the rain on James Garfield's famous log* instead of behind a desk. They couldn't have cared less.

The high school grads of the "medium" precincts followed the Golden Mean recommended by certain of the great philosophers. That is, they split down the middle on the proposition and settled for a tie. Such action, of course, solves nothing and exasperates everybody, but it does follow the impressive precedent which our government has set in its last two wars of going all out and gung-ho for a rousing standoff.

It remained for the ignorant and largely uneducated "low" voters to pull the schools' financial chestnuts out of the fire. They came through like the U.S. cavalry in a John Wayne epic with a resounding "yes" which carried the measure to a narrow victory. And this despite the un-

* That pestiferous log of Garfield's, now an ineradicable fixture of American educational folklore, never really existed. Here is what Garfield really said, in an address to Williams College alumni in New York, Dec. 28, 1871 (Page 652, Bartlett's Familiar Quotations, 13th edition): "Give me a log hut, with only a simple bench, Mark Hopkins on one end and I on the other, and you may have all the buildings, apparatus and libraries without him."

doubted fact that they had received less from the schools than anyone else and had less reason to support them.

Now before anyone starts chiding me for leaping frantically to conclusions, let me hasten to point out that obviously a lot of other factors were to be found in this situation.

Of course the "high" voters were also those with the most property to tax and, therefore, were the ones who would have had to pay most.

And of course there's the point that a lot of the college folks had their offspring enrolled in private schools and thus were already paying twice for education.

Then too there just might have been a hidden flaw in the bond proposal which only the sharpies in the "high" precincts could see through.

Somehow I doubt it. But whatever the motives involved, the implications for education are almost too ghastly to contemplate.

Apparently the more education the public gets, the less apt it is to support education.

And since we schoolmen have long been trying to educate everybody to his maximum potential, we are now faced with the horrendous possibility that we are working ourselves right out of our jobs. Maybe we'd be better off to hold everyone to the grammar school level, thus ensuring at least the survival of public education in the United States.

This way lies madness. Like Scarlett O'Hara, I prefer to think about it tomorrow.

But somebody had better be thinking about it. And that "somebody," I trust, will be the "high" voter. It's not the fault of us teachers that the American people are breeding immoderately and flooding the schools with unprecedented numbers of children. If you're going to keep on sending us all these kids, you'd better plan to send the money along with them, at least to put roofs over their heads.

And please don't tell me you voted "no" in a school bond election as a protest against a frivolous or fatuous educational philosophy.

That's about as sensible as refusing to build a garage for your car because you don't approve of smog.

THE GOOD OLD SUMMERTIME
*And if you want to know who's responsible
for school not running the year 'round, just
look in the mirror . . .*

As the dog days approach, the seasonal crop of indignant letters about a longer school year begins to ripen and burgeon. Some of my friends in the business world have a pretty low boiling point anyway, and the sight of an expensive school building sitting maddeningly idle as they drive brow-moppingly past it on a hot summer's day seems to bring out the H. L. Mencken even in the most Babbitt-like businessman.

"Don't you ivory-tower educators realize the amount of money tied up in those empty school plants?" asks one plaintive critic. "I don't mind having my tax money go to pay teachers for working, but I seriously object to paying for their three-month vacation every year."

Another gentleman asks cuttingly: "What would you

think if General Motors shut down for three months every summer? Where would you get your tax revenue?"

Simmer down, fellows.

When General Motors, plus all the rest of you, start giving one-fourth of your vacations in the summer, one-fourth in the fall, one-fourth in the winter and one-fourth in the spring, then we school people will be glad to do the same with the kids. Right now, more than 75% of all industrial and business vacations are set for the months of June, July and August.

Should the schools follow your advice unilaterally, here's what would happen:

Pop jockeys the station wagon into the home driveway, exulting in the prospect of a two-week hunting and fishing trek into the High Sierras with Junior. He loads the fishing tackle into the back end, packs the tent on top and puts the .30-.30 on the floor. Then he whistles for Junior to hop in and get going—and right there trouble starts.

Junior comes slowly out of the house, woe and despair written all over him.

"I can't go this summer, Pop," he sobs. "Principal Smith says I have to stay in school."

I shall draw a charitable veil over the rest of this scene, except to note that Pop is all too apt to get the .30-.30 out of the car and go looking for Principal Smith. People have the possibly quaint idea that children ought to go on vacations with their parents, you see.

What we school men would much rather see is a vast expansion of the present, very healthy, voluntary summer-school program. Some schools give courses which offer credit toward graduation, and a youngster can actually graduate from high school in three and a half years instead of four if he wants to spend some time in summer school every year.

Such a plan changes our vignette drastically:

Pop comes home, loads the car and whistles for Junior. But this time Junior says firmly: "I'm not going this year. If I go to summer school, I can get out of high school in February instead of June, and I can use the time I save earning enough money so that you won't have to pay for my first year's tuition at State University."

You'd be surprised at the difference this makes in the old man's attitude. He's apt to take Mom along on the hunting trip instead, which may be just as well, too.

I've worked in schools where more than 60% of the pupils were in school almost 11 months out of the year, instead of nine. They were there because they wanted to be, or at least because their parents wanted them to be—not because they were compelled by law.

And what a difference that one little factor makes, especially to the teacher. Just the difference between a summer in a seminar and a summer in Sing Sing.

You see, in the final analysis, education is for people who really want it, not for those who have to be clubbed into submitting to it. In a way, it's too bad that summer school can't last all year long.

The Gifted

Strange youngsters. Sometimes troublesome. Withdrawn. Often impatient. Even rude.

The days beyond tomorrow are theirs . . .

GIFTEDNESS AND GENIUS: THE GULF BETWEEN
*There's only one safe generalization which can
be made about the genius. He's usually a hard
man to get along with . . .*

How many of your friends are mentally gifted? Mind you,
I'm not asking how many THINK they are. I'm asking how
many really are.

Several, perhaps, if you're lucky.

How many geniuses do you know? Almost certainly
none.

The so-called I.Q. scale is like a thermometer. It starts
theoretically at zero, but actually no one could have zero
intelligence and live at all. Idiocy hovers around the 20
mark, shading upward imperceptibly into imbecility around
40. The low-grade moron has an I.Q. in the 50s or 60s, and
normal intelligence occupies the broad sector of the spectrum between 90 and 110.

It's in the rarefied upper reaches of the scale that the
prosy, humdrum world which most of us inhabit undergoes a subtle sea-change into something strange and new.
Giftedness starts around 130, and then the I.Q. elevator
heads for the stratosphere with fewer and fewer passengers

aboard until it clangs to a virtually unheard stop at the mythical top floor of 200.

But by that time, like the deep space probes, it has left humanity behind.

Somewhere in the exclusive neighborhood of 170, that elusive, incomprehensible thing called genius takes over, and right there the human race loses contact with its own peculiar and often tormented stepchildren. Always they have been so few in number that each genius has lived his life in almost total isolation from his own kind, often in a purgatory of loneliness impossible for the rest of us to even imagine.

After all, how could we? Can the unfortunate imbecile understand us normals, solve our problems, share our interests, dream our dreams? Yet the true genius is as far above us on the mental scale as we are above the imbecile, and his world is as inconceivably dissimilar. The gifted are faster, more efficient versions of ourselves. We can figure out what makes them tick. The genius is—different.

Try to imagine yourself in a society where everybody else is feeble-minded. Picture the infinity of slack jaws, vacant eyes, untied shoelaces, senseless gabble. Pretty frightening, isn't it?

The plight of the genius is not exactly comparable, but it must be almost as bleak. No wonder so many of them down through the ages have burned forlornly at the stakes of ignorance and superstition or have beaten their priceless brains out against the walls of madhouse cells.

No one knows what genius really is. It's not high I.Q. alone. It has been inadequately defined as the ability to solve problems without knowing how, to arrive at the right answer without going through any visible process of logical reasoning. But I can tell you how to recognize the genius. Look for the twin stigmata of impatience and frustration. They are at once his hallmark and his albatross.

Genius is Leonardo da Vinci dying in the arms of the king of France, moaning that he had neglected all his opportunities.

It's Beethoven shaking his fist impatiently at the heavens themselves.

It's Moses shattering in mute rage the Tablets of the Law.

How many geniuses of this stamp are alive today? Probably not more than 50 out of all the burgeoning billions of our planetary population. And of these, half are doubtless "mute inglorious Miltons," unknown, unrecognized, unheeded.

The genius makes the rest of us uncomfortable, as what we do not understand will always set our teeth on edge. He is generally odd, frequently enigmatic, often cross-grained and hard to get along with.

Yet once in a generation or so, like a supernova bursting upon a darkly quiet summer sky, he comes to us from nowhere, lifting us against our will out of the comfortable rut which we have dug for ourselves, carrying us with him as though on seven-league boots into a future which he not only discerns but also helps, giant-like, to shape.

In my profession we do not yet know how to school a genius. We may never know. But it is not too much to hope that we educators may yet learn to identify him at an early age, to understand a little of the strange, bright, harried world in which he lives and moves, and above all to give him elbowroom.

HOW NOT TO TREAT THE BRAINY
*And there's an equally safe generalization which
can be made about a teacher of the gifted.
He'd better be gifted too . . .*

Let me share with you a letter from an agonized parent:

"Our daughter has an I.Q. of 133. She is gifted. Her high school, wishing to encourage its above-average students to practice excellence, organized them into honors classes. Everybody in these classes was gifted. As a result, some got C's, some B's, a few A's. Since my gifted daughter, who was competing through high school with other children even more gifted than she, got a couple of C grades, she has recently been turned down by the university of her choice. Is this fair?"

No, ma'am. You can bet your mortarboard it isn't fair. In fact, it's pretty close to an outrage.

In a case like this, it is a kind of dreary tossup as to which institution has behaved in the more clod-pated, doltish, downright irresponsible manner: the high school which insisted upon grading its priceless gifted "on the curve" or the university which stupidly treated honors-course graduates just the same as other applicants for admission.

The purpose of a high school honors course, is to offer subjects and classes of special depth and complexity for the few students intelligent enough to need this kind of challenge. Screening for such classes is usually on the threefold basis of I.Q., past grades and teacher recommendations.

Only a very small precentage of the student body—sometimes only the upper 2%—will be eligible for honors-course enrollment.

Now, since we have a clear choice as a people of selecting our future leaders from the smart or the stupid, and since it is pretty obvious which group we ought to be training for such leadership, it therefore follows as the night the day that high school honors classes of some kind or other are a good thing and ought to be encouraged, not kicked in the teeth by a blockheaded institutional bureaucracy.

A high school should do one of two things: it should either clear its honors courses with all reputable institutions of higher learning, with a guarantee of special treatment by admissions officers of honors-course graduates with C grades, or it should see that its instructors give nothing but A and B grades to honors-course enrollees.

And in case anyone has any lingering reservations about the desirability of this sort of grading, let me present you with a ridiculously hypothetical but nonetheless meaningful dilemma:

Suppose you are a science teacher, with a class consisting entirely of Isaac Newton, Albert Einstein, Archimedes, Louis Pasteur, Benjamin Franklin, Thomas Edison, Marie Curie, Jonas Salk and Leonardo da Vinci. To which ones will you give C grades, thus keeping them from going on to college?

You could do it, you know, by keeping numerical grade scores on written objective tests, translating total averages into grade-point equivalents carried down to four decimal places and then arbitrarily applying the normal curve of statistical distribution to determine who get the C's.

Yes, you could do it, all right. But if you did, you would be an idiot. Worse, you could be depriving society of such useful bagatelles as the theory of gravity, polio vaccine, relativity, the electric light, atomic energy, pasteurized milk and several others. Viewed in this light, you would be the biggest public enemy since Hitler.

If I were teaching the group I just dreamed up, I would give every one of them an A. If I were teaching any real honors class, I would give everyone in it an A or a B. If anyone had got into the class by mistake, and didn't rate honors grades, I'd see that he got back into a more orthodox group of mixed abilities.

Let's not penalize the honors students. We have none too many as it is. Those we do have may be required to save our bacon 20 years from now.

Morality and Religion

Schools have always existed to teach children what is good and right.

Despite the outcries of the New Immoralists, things haven't changed.

At least, they'd better not change.

THE NEED FOR SEX EDUCATION

There's more to sex education than facts and techniques. There's a little matter of morality . . .

At first glance it would seem that today's children need instruction in sexual matters about as much as Custer needed more Indians. From the time they get up in the morning and examine the comic strips until the time they go to bed at night, groggy from the late, late show, they are fed an almost unmixed diet of high-calorie, highly commercialized sex.

With the honorable exception of Walt Disney and a very few others, the motion picture producers confront the kids with a succession of dismal, dreadful themes ranging from incest to sodomy, with once in a while a little good old-fashioned cannibalism thrown in, just to keep them on their toes.

The so-called legitimate stage has achieved a condition of such sheer filth as to merit the adjective "indescribable." We are the first generation since time began which has allowed its playwrights and its actors to wallow in vileness. True, Restoration Drama in the days of Charles II was pretty gamy, but it was by all odds a healthier, more natural sort of game. Charles, after all, was known as a merry monarch, not a sick one.

The novel today is rapidly becoming a refuge for pathological deviations described in four-letter words. The pocket books on display at our newsstands look as though they had been culled from one of King Farouk's collections. And advertising is making rapid progress toward its ultimate goal of reducing everything—from razor blades to root beer—to one common denominator: sex.

As a result of all this, we are seeing in our time and among our children a veritable explosion of all sorts of unpleasant things, from illegitimate pregnancies to venereal disease. So a lot of people are urging the schools to step in and clean this mess up by giving the youngsters a good, stiff dose of sex education.

I am the last person in the world to come out against any kind of education, but I think we'd better take a long look at the major premise. Proponents of mass compulsory instruction in this field assume that knowledge of principles and techniques will in itself solve the problem.

I doubt it.

People are not discouraged from becoming safecrackers by learning how to manipulate tumblers in the dark. They avoid a life of crime because they are taught from infancy that crime is evil.

Similarly, I don't think we are going to crack the sex delinquency puzzle by seeing that all the kids understand the mechanics of sex. The only way society has ever found to discourage misconduct is to label it clearly as either a crime or a sin, or both, and then punish it accordingly.

Until we as a people recognize openly the ancient truth that illicit and premarital sex is an offense against both God and man, if only because of its chilling selfishness and complete disregard for others, we will not see the current situation improve.

Sex education for high schoolers, with the written consent of their parents and under conditions of scientific objectivity, may add to their sum total of knowledge about themselves and thus do good. But it will not in itself answer the riddle with which we are confronted.

The riddle is this: How can the schools unilaterally solve a problem which originates outside the schools and which permeates society as a whole?

And the answer is: They cannot. Only when we adults, in our homes, our churches, our businesses, decide that we are going to set a decent example and demand decent behavior from the young will the children start growing up to become the kind of people we want them to be, and should have been ourselves.

NEEDED: A NEW HIPPOCRATIC OATH
Physician, heal thyself . . .

What in blazes is getting into some of our medical doctors these days?

Not that all the Kildares and Caseys have been pillars of eternal virtue. Over the years the docs have had their share of quacks and rogues. But by and large the men with the little black bags are pretty decent fellows: family men, PTA members, patriotic Americans. Above all, the ones

I've known have loved children—their own and everybody else's.

That's why I'm puzzled about the recent antics of a few of America's medicos; puzzled and interested in what the overwhelmingly moral majority of this great profession elects to do about its minuscule, but offensive, lunatic fringe.

The practitioner I'd like to pounce on here is a certain college physician who announced proudly that he had begun passing out contraceptives to coeds. I'll admit I have had a few doubts about this particular eastern institution of allegedly higher learning, but these have now been completely resolved by this simpering statement from the head of its student clinic. Its administrators have got to have rocks in their heads.

I am all for international birth control, what with the earth's population doubling every 30 years or so, but I question seriously whether Mom and Pop are dipping into the family nest-egg to send Susie to dear old Ribald U. so that she can study the problem first-hand. "Learning by doing" was an educational principle dear to John Dewey's heart, but I gravely doubt that he had sex in mind when he enunciated it.

You took the oath of Hippocrates, Doc, before you got your shingle. Did it exhort you to abet immorality, or to inhibit it?

Instead of smoothing and prettying up the primrose path for Susie with your handy little scientific gadgets, did it ever occur to you to give her some unscientific but helpful hell when she came into your office to seek assistance in her sinning?

Above all, is it too much to ask a college doctor to talk about decency and morality and virtue to a college girl when he sees her getting ready to take the first false step?

Your attitude of laissez-faire and Olympian broadmindedness as you dispense your medical "Helpful Hints to Careless Coeds" might perhaps be appropriate for a consultant physician on Red Light Row, Doc, but it's as out of place in a school as a 3-unit course in "How to Use Burglar Tools."

When I send a daughter to college and spend a small fortune to get her graduated, I don't intend for her to get her degree in debauchery. If she's set on debauching, let her do it without the tacit sanction of the college authorities and the open assistance of the college physician. I expect something a little more constructive than this from you, gentlemen, when I scrape up the $8,000 or so to put her through your ivied institution.

On second thought, I guess I shouldn't be too surprised at the antics of an errant doctor or two, particularly when I meditate upon the fatheadedness of some of my fellow educators.

For instance, there's the dean of women in one of our most exclusive western universities who reported to her president that some of the English professors were seducing their better-looking female students as a sort of extracurricular bonus added to their regular emoluments.

The president was understandably annoyed. Even upset. But he solved the problem in short order.

He fired the dean of women.

LEARNING BY DOING—NEW STYLE
Once again, just because cyanide is a fact of life,
it's not necessary to serve it to kids merely
to prove how broad-minded we are . . .

We educators get accused of so many things these days that it's almost a relief to find a member of one of our sister professions making an ass of himself. Misery loves company, I suppose.

At any rate, a medical doctor heading a commission on the study of alcoholism in one of our larger states came out the other day with a recommendation that school children be taught how to drink liquor. He feels they are going to grow up to be drinkers anyway, so they might as well learn how to do it properly down in the grades.

This opens up a whole new vista for my profession, of course. Think of the possibilities.

Ten per cent of the adult population require mental treatment in some institution before they die, so say the statistics. Presumably, the schools should equip an equivalent percentage of classrooms with padded walls, barred windows and strait-jackets, so the kids can learn how to behave properly when the law of averages catches up with them and remands them to a mental home.

An increasing proportion of us rely on barbiturates, pep pills, hypnotic drugs and goof balls to get us through the rigors of a typical 20th-century day. Obviously, our primary grade teachers should acquire at least a minor in pharmacy so they can prescribe just the right daily dosage to the little ones with their 10 o'clock milk. Then when the children grow up they will be numbed enough to keep them from worrying about school taxes, but not too numbed to prevent them from paying.

And if we are to have education for drinking, why not for marijuana smoking, too? They tell me it's considered less addictive than the cup that cheers, and since some of the small fry will no doubt become reefer puffers as they grow older, surely we should teach everybody how to inhale that "tea" with verve and eclat.

All right, I'm being ridiculous. But the good doctor was being ridiculous, too. And don't tell me he meant well. I know he meant well. He was following the age-old precedent set by the 18th-century English squires, the "two-bottle men" of Fielding's day, who taught their sons at an early age to "drink like gentlemen," thus raising generation after generation of drunkards, to the delight of Hogarth and the despair of the clergy.

Teaching youngsters how to drink properly didn't work then. It won't work now. Kids should be taught about alcohol, right enough: what it is, how it works, whom it kills and why it has become big business. The laws of my state require every teacher to instruct his pupils in "the evils of alcohol." That's right: "evils." Just like that—with no ifs, ands or buts.

It is possible, of course, that the sliding, mushy, collapsing moral standards of our time will some day force a change in the wording of this sublimely simple statute. But until they do I suggest that we continue to warn the kids away from John Barleycorn, not introduce them to him as a jovial companion down in the grades.

I suppose I'll hear now from every antibluenose in the

land—reviling me for being a Puritan and comparing me to every humorless nut from Carry Nation to Anthony Comstock. So be it. My concern is with the little ones, and I don't care if every doctor on every alcoholism commission in the country pooh-poohs me as a hopeless square.

Schools are not built or maintained to compromise with evil. And teaching children to drink is evil, no matter how you slice it.

Go ahead, you social drinkers, and enjoy your martinis. Offer me one. Maybe I'll take it. But I won't share it with Junior. Nor do I want his school to do so.

I'll probably enjoy the drink. But I won't kid myself into thinking it's good for me. I suggest we keep the schools out of the kidding business, too.

'LIFE ADJUSTMENT' EDUCATION VERSUS NATIONAL SURVIVAL
A diffident suggestion that if our ancestors were
to return to earth unexpectedly, they would give
us a swift kick in the pants . . .

Time for a couple of what the movies used to call "short subjects." Lights! Action! Camera!

1—The year is 1778. A drunken Hessian mercenary has taken nine American girls prisoner all by himself and just told them collectively to line up and shut up while he cuts their throats individually with his bayonet.

Question: Do the colonial girls fall into line meekly, like so many sheep, and without even uttering a bleat of protest permit this liquored-up psychotic to slaughter them all, one by one? Or do they swarm all over him like enraged Amazons and initiate a little throat-cutting on their own?

2—It's 100 years later, and a lone Apache renegade has ordered 13 able-bodied frontier women to lie down clock-wise so he can shoot them all to death at his leisure.

Question: Do our pioneer mothers lie down quietly and give up? Or do they clobber this junior-grade Geronimo with everything but the kitchen sink, screaming all the while like a bevy of banshees?

You know perfectly well what our ancestresses would have done, don't you? In each of the conjectured cases above, the male criminal would have done well to get away approximately in one piece and with even a few remaining wisps of hair.

Oh, he might have stabbed or shot one or two of the aroused ladies during the hassle, but the rest of them would have beaten, bruised and bloodied him to a pulp.

And if one of our great-great-grandfathers had chanced to wander in on either scene described above, he would have promptly bent his long rifle double around the mur-derer's neck, and the whole community would have turned out to string up what was left of the offender.

Yet anyone who follows the news must know that the trend today is running strongly toward co-operating doc-ilely with these sneering, sadistic savages while they are about their bloody business and then treating them as sweetly as possible, if and when they are apprehended.

Just substitute nine intern nurses back east for the co-lonial girls in Vignette No. 1 and 13 Arizona beauty-parlor patrons for the pioneer women in Case No. 2, and you'll see in a hurry the almost 180-degree change in our national attitude toward survival which the passing of a couple of generations has brought about.

What caused it?

Oh, a lot of things, as is usually the case with a mass change of attitudes and values. But I'd be inclined to give a good deal of the credit to the cult of "life adjustment" education which took over the nation's schools around 1935.

Over the years, our children have been taught in their classrooms to adjust to their environment at any cost, to attach top importance to easy, comfortable, happy acceptance by their peer group and to avoid that nasty word "competition" like the plague.

Draw the charmed circle wide enough to let everybody and everything in, one way or the other. Strive always for compromise and consensus, never for victory. Distrust corny old shibboleths like honor and piety. Attach top priority to groupism, never to individual initiative and gumption.

This is an important part of the gospel according to St. John Dewey. But it is more than that. Over the long haul of history it is a recipe for national suicide because it teaches the small fry the supreme virtue of seeking accommodation with those whose sworn, remorseless intention is to destroy us utterly.

In the past when an American was confronted by naked evil brandishing an ax, he went after it tooth and claw and to the devil with the consequences. He destroyed it root and branch, or he died trying.

Today we are more apt to appoint a fact-finding committee. Or, better yet, get the Supreme Court to modify the current definition of the word "evil." It helps so much to know that the fellow who's busy dismembering you isn't really bad at all. Just socially maladjusted.

IT MAY NOT BE A MAD, MAD WORLD, BUT IT'S TRYING HARD
We used to lock up the loose nuts. Now we let
them put on exhibitions, or even preach to us
on Sunday . . .

Maybe old Cicero felt the way I do when he was giving Catiline the "O tempora! O mores!" bit. I don't know. But every so often these days I am overcome with the qualmish feeling that I am living in some kind of planetary nut-house.

And unlike the late Robert Benchley who used to deal with the occasional and irrational urge to exercise by sitting down firmly until the impulse went away, I prefer to achieve catharsis by putting my own fears into writing, just to see whether anybody else shares this Alice-in-Wonderland vertigo with me.

For instance:

My own profession is being badgered and plagued increasingly by the sad-sack addicts of the so-called hallucinatory drugs. In fact, on the Pacific Coast where things are not always what they seem you can now go to "happenings" where the audience can experience all the effects of LSD without actually ingesting the stuff.

Some paint-smeared moron will crawl stark naked along a king-size strip of paper, while another lackwit will considerately tip over a 50-gallon tin of jelly for the spectators to eat and/or wallow in. Unearthly lights and earsplitting sounds are then turned loose to sandpaper whatever nerve endings may still be left, and the end product is a reasonable facsimile of Saturday night in a communal padded cell.

It wouldn't be so bad if a lot of kids hadn't become addicted to this bilge. As it is, some of them are coming to school on Monday expecting class to be a "happening," too. Pity the poor pedagog! It was tough enough trying to compete with compact cars, outdoor movies, color TV and the Beatles. But the current craving for psychedelic schoolhouses is ridiculous.

Then, entirely on another level of irrationality, there is the misty-eyed, choked-up adoration which most of our Negro leaders seem to feel for the ineffable Adam Clayton Powell. Every time someone turns over another odorous page in the life history of the Casanova of the Greater Antilles, almost the entire Negro community leaps galvanically to his defense, for all the world as though this nepotistic Lothario were the original inventor of the Negro old-school tie.

It's exactly as though the white power structure 10 years ago had rallied wild-eyed and slogan-shouting around the bedraggled person of the late Errol Flynn.

Finally, there are a couple of my own Episcopal Church colleagues, who, to put it mildly, are not making education's job any easier.

Bishop James Pike, in a rare interval between heresy charges, found time to warn his government that unless it heeds his advice on foreign policy there will be wholesale defiance of the draft by American youth, presumably with his fatherly blessing. The good bishop has thus gone the

Founder of his faith one better by ordering Caesar to render unto him.

And another eminent Anglican theologian, Prof. Joseph Fletcher, announced in the kind of stentorian tones formerly reserved for the breaking of the seals in the Book of Revelation: "Sex is clearly in the category of recreation. In sex, we call freedom 'love.' In politics, we call it democracy.'"

In short, fellow squares, we now find ourselves in a box where if we preach continence and virginity to our own children we run the risk of being denounced from the pulpit as undemocratic. This equation of free love with free speech and free press would, I'm sure, have intrigued T. Jefferson and A. Jackson no end, and when carried to its logical conclusion will no doubt result in the election of *Playboy* magazine's Hugh Hefner to the Presidency one of these days.

Ah, well. If my cool deserts me completely, I can always claim I'm either on a "trip" or at a "happening."

Except that to me this kind of unmitigated balderdash is an open invitation to wholesale recruitment for the local booby hatch. But who am I to stand up to the clergy, the professors and the students in serried ranks aligned? In a not-too-distant world where sanity is only what a revved-up, twitching, psychedelic society says it is, I'm liable to be a likely candidate for the funny farm myself.

Okay, fellows. You won't need the nets. I'll go quietly.

EDUCATION AND THE 'NEW MORALITY'
*This may come as a shock, but there are still
such things as "right" and "wrong." And not
only in answers to arithmetic problems,
either . . .*

Sometimes I think the best man to be United States commissioner of education would be Billy Graham.

More and more we are seeing that the main problems
the schools face today are moral ones. From sex education
to slobbism, from discipline to decency, from patriotism
to pornography, we educators are confronted almost daily
with bizarre and even creepy puzzles stemming from somebody's insatiable desire to uproot the ethical standards of
2000 years and to substitute for them the moral criteria of
a pack of sex-starved alley cats. For instance:

How can a high school teacher expose her English class
to so-called "modern" literature without simultaneously
violating not only state laws prohibiting profanity and
obscenity in the classroom, but also the ordinary canons
of person-to-person seemliness?

Do we teach youngsters to avoid premarital sexual inter-
course because it is morally wrong or because it's apt to
make the participants either syphilitic or pregnant or occasionally both? You'd be surprised how much difference
of opinion there is on this one. Or maybe you wouldn't.

Are we to teach children to obey all laws or just some of
them? And if the latter, then shall we introduce courses of
study designed to enable kids to distinguish between "good"
laws and "bad" ones?

Shall we advise the next generation to uphold our country in its dealings with the rest of the world or only when, in the individual's opinion, his country happens to be "right"? In other words, do we love our native land all the time or only when we happen to agree with her?

These are just a few of the everyday questions that educators are being called upon to cope with, and the coping is not being made any easier by the unheard-of roadblocks currently being placed in our path by individuals and groups who in the past had always been our staunchest allies and who certainly ought to know better even today.

Some time ago we were regaled with a simultaneous statement from several prominent members of the clergy to the effect that God had suddenly died. Since this breathless revelation, I've been waiting for the follow-up announcement that these men of the cloth had resigned from their jobs and had gone into some other calling, for the same reason that the manufacturers of buggy whips changed their vocation after the demise of the surrey and the hansom cab.

But no. Apparently it's going to take enough time to wind up God's affairs to enable these evangelists of nothingness to hang onto their parishes and pass the collection plate every Sunday with a clear conscience. Bless them. I don't know *who* will bless them now, but bless them anyway.

Then there was the nationally known character who described himself modestly as an "author, poet and teacher" when he trumpeted his latest book, *The Sexual Revolution*, as the first positive treatment of the New Morality. In this piece of deathless prose, he advocates "experimenting with the new," and to facilitate such experimentation he wants to abolish all laws dealing with morality.

His vision of a brave new world satiated with sodomy, primed with pornography and luxuriant with lubricity would never have made me feel much like Keats' watcher of the skies when some new planet swims into his ken, but normally I can take this sort of goatishness in stride.

This time I was at a disadvantage. I had just eaten.

Even then I wouldn't have minded the author's paean to pruriency if he had not in the same breath called himself a teacher. That did it.

What are we educators to do when preachers, librarians and even some of our own fellow professionals seem determined to embrace this new cult of moral and intellectual nihilism? Are we obliged willy-nilly to join in the chorus of "Anything Goes"?

Not if we want to continue as a profession. Parents pay us to introduce their children to the accumulated culture, wisdom and refinement of the ages, not to give them a mud bath in vice and suggestiveness. They expect us to inspire in those children a love for the good, the true and the beautiful.

Anybody can pick up obscenity and irreverence on any street corner. You don't have to go to school to learn four-letter words and ugly racial slurs. The schools are built and supported to fight against this sort of dry rot, not to go over to it and embrace it.

We teachers need to set standards, understand them and then uphold them. And this we cannot do until we abandon an educational philosophy which holds that all standards are fictitious and all truths mere fantasy.

EDUCATION IS NOT SUPERMAN—NOT EVEN BATMAN
*Sometimes it's a good idea to define our
limitations . . .*

There's a myth currently flitting about the country like an unidentified flying object to the effect that education can do anything.

The sentiment is almost always hedged carefully about with such qualifying phrases as "given the necessary climate of support" and "under proper leadership," but the gist of the argument is that in education we have a newly discovered national magic wand unequaled since Cinderella's fairy godmother solved the domestic servant shortage and the transportation problem while simultaneously reducing the rodent population.

This legend relates to and in fact closely resembles the even more widely accepted myth that American money is the universal panacea for all our existing evils from ax murders to Appalachia. Here the "magic wand" psychology is both warmly embraced and assiduously propagated by the bureaucracy in Washington and is perfectly understandable in the light of its past success with other magic acts such as the disappearance of the gold from Fort Knox and the silver from our coins.

What bothers me about the education myth is that in many cases it is being spread by educators who certainly ought to know better. There is no question, that good schooling can work modest wonders. There is every question that it can work immodest miracles.

For example:

1—Education alone cannot make anyone a better human being, change a villain to a hero nor transform an irresponsible nincompoop into a sober, constructive citizen. The schools in my state all teach driver education, and most of them teach it very well, but there is no evidence to date that by so doing they have reduced either the collective death-wish or the mortality rate among these teen-age dimwits who insist upon drag racing lethally and playing "chicken" on the county highway at midnight.

Similarly we teachers have seen that every member of the rising generation knows all about the horrendous effects of tobacco and alcohol, but as of this writing we have not observed any decline in the use of these two delightful destroyers.

2—Education cannot guarantee a man a job. It can give him the skills he needs to get and hold a job; the all-important attitude and desire he must generate himself.

3—Education cannot create leaders. Only God can do that.

4—Education cannot prevent wars. Germany in the Thirties was the best-educated land in Europe. Education is like nuclear energy in this respect. Its potential can be used either for good or for evil. The atavistic itch to fight is what causes wars, and with such deep-buried urges education is simply not designed to deal.

And so it goes. The common denominator in all these "cannots" is the inability of education alone to make people want to do what's good for them. It can give Americans the facts. It can teach them how to organize those facts. It can even build up certain desirable work habits and patterns of stimulus-response. But it cannot, merely by presenting the good, the true, the beautiful to its captive audience, necessarily make its pupils hanker after these fine old attributes.

What a lot of people fail to realize is that the schools are up against some pretty stiff competition these days.

The novels tell the world in four-letter words that every hero is in reality a villain, and vice-versa.

The stage glorifies the "un-man," the spiritual amputee, the adult crybaby who blubbers about the 20th century without having the guts to try to improve it.

The movies are as sniggeringly and tastelessly vile as a stag party after the guests have become maudlin enough to hiccup barnyard quips at the overweight and somewhat jaundiced stripteaser.

Television should be commented upon only by authorities on the mentally retarded.

We educators, in short, are doing our darndest to maintain an oasis of values in a desert of sometimes sparkling and occasionally seductive slop. But it would be unreasonable to expect us unilaterally to reclaim the entire Sahara.

AFTER ALL, WHO WANTS $200 MILLION?
*An uncomprehending stare at the muck
merchants . . .*

Time out while I gratify an ancient urge and act as movie critic.

No one, least of all an educator, likes to see one of education's main doors slammed shut and barred right smack in the face of the children. That's why I'm zeroing in today on Hollywood's movie producers, and a crazy, mixed-up bunch they are.

If any of you have a 14-year-old child, as I do, you know exactly what I'm talking about. We parents used to be able to bundle the kids off to the neighborhood theater on Saturday with a reasonable assurance that they wouldn't be relentlessly bombarded for three hours with enough rape, incest and stomach-turning perversion to make Sodom and Gomorrah look like Disneyland by comparison and that they might even soak up some interesting incidental facts about history, geography and human affairs.

Not any more.

Nowadays before any halfway conscientious Mom and Pop dare send an offspring to see a show they have to curl up for a prolonged session with *Parents' Magazine* or the National Office for Motion Pictures bulletin to try and find something they can expose Junior to which won't turn him into a raving sex maniac. And this has become such a chore that most of us currently are throwing up our hands in despair and either unleashing a panting Junior to go see Susan Smut in *Lust Alley* or refusing point-blank to let him go to any movie at all.

Either choice is a bad one. Just as either is cowardly. What really raises my hackles is that we parents find ourselves in such a bind that we have to opt for one or the other.

I hasten to add that it is not just personal pique that's biting me in regard to the movie makers. I'm seriously concerned about their sanity.

For instance:

The last box-office returns I got a good look at listed

My Fair Lady, Mary Poppins and *The Sound of Music* as far and away the biggest money-makers of the past five years. Rumor even has it that the last-named blockbuster may well rack up the absolutely astounding take of $200 million, a figure which would put *The Sound of Music* so many light-years ahead of all competitors past and present that it would occupy a special, diamond-studded, uranium-lined category all its own in the annals of moviedom.

With its two worthy companion films it occupies another almost unique category, too. It's clean. I mean, really. No dry rot around the edges. No leering obscenities or double entendres. No sick obsessions.

How can it possibly make so much money? Isn't it hopelessly corny? And everybody knows corn is "out" with the "in" group these days.

The critics, at least, assure us of this solemnly every time they write a column. True to their bilious form they have hurled all kinds of dead cats at "The Sound of Music."

"Treacly," one of them sniffed distastefully.

"Banal and goody-goody," another pontificated.

This I can understand, because I understand critics. But the wise guys among my producer friends are fond of sneering at the Julie Andrews opus, too. And this I *cannot* understand at all. After all, the critics don't get a cut of the gate receipts, but the producers are very much in business to make money.

How can anybody sneer at $200 million? Especially producers?

When the three great grossers of the Sixties are all spotless in plot and dialog, somebody just has to be wrong about what American audiences want. And I think that "somebody" is Hollywood. The moral to this story is apparently that you can turn a few fast and filthy bucks by pandering to the rottenness which all of us have a little of, but if you want to make $200 million you'd better play up to the decency which is a lot more characteristic of the American people. Whether Hollywood thinks so or not.

I know better than to appeal to our movie moguls' morality or sense of responsibility or sheer seemliness. But I should think that money would talk. And loudly.

In the past, where most of these characters are concerned, it's the only thing that has.

WHATEVER HAPPENED TO SUNDAY SCHOOL?
And a jaundiced eye cast Sunday School-ward. . . .

In discussing Red China's popularity nose-dive stemming from some of Mao's more senile speeches, I happened to mention to an honors class in history that this marked the first time since Samson that the jawbone of an ass had produced such devastating results.

You would have thought I was speaking Sanscrit. The boys eyed one another blankly, and the girls giggled dutifully, apparently believing I had cracked some particularly esoteric joke. So I decided to grasp the nettle firmly.

"What do I mean by a coat of many colors?" I inquired dulcetly. No one knew.

"Manna from heaven?" I asked hopefully. The class began to manifest grave anxiety, so I plunged hastily to my final question.

"How many of you have gone to Sunday school?"

Practically everybody, as it turned out. A good many of them had been regular attendants until they got into high school. Some of them even had silver attendance medals which they kindly offered to bring the next day in case I didn't believe them.

I believed them. What I didn't—and don't—believe is that any of them learned anything while they were attending. Except how to color the lost sheep black and Esau's beard brown in the coloring books, of course, while memorizing at a somewhat earlier age the words to "Jesus Wants Me for a Sunbeam."

I get a considerable kick out of some of our fine parochial-school people who rib me about alleged superficiality and some downright puerility in the public school curriculum.

What about the curriculum in their own Sunday schools? In nine cases out of 10 it is so inept, shallow and foolishly piddling that it makes even the most blitheringly "progressive" of our public schools look like Caltech by comparison. It's a shame, too, because Sunday school can be and should be an important force in literary as well as religious education.

The Ark of the Covenant. Ruth in tears amid the alien corn. The sword of the Lord and of Gideon. The waters of Babylon. The patience of Job. Jonah and the whale. David and Goliath.

I don't care whether a child is destined to be a Jew, Catholic, Protestant, Black Muslim, Holy Roller or ranting atheist. If he is ever to advance the slightest claim to being an educated man he simply has to be intimately familiar with these and hundreds of other sublime stories which are the legendary landmarks of our whole Western civilization. To go through life ignorant of the great Bible tales is to hobble hamstrung down a darkened course with blinders on.

And if a youngster doesn't get this material in Sunday school, where is he going to get it?

Not at home. Family reading is rapidly becoming a lost art, thanks to the boob tube and "community recreation."

Not at school. The average teacher is scared stiff even to mention the Bible in class, thanks to a Supreme Court which beams benevolently upon its own child-marrying mountain climbers but which consistently hands down decisions designed to nip in the bud any attempts to elevate moral and spiritual values in the public schools.

Only in Sunday school can tomorrow's generation be exposed systematically to the treasures embedded in the world's greatest book. And I'm not talking about religious treasures. I am talking about cultural treasures.

Don't take my word for what's going on. Try these questions on your own kids:

Who denied he was his brother's keeper?

What happened to Lot's wife?

Who ate the original mess of pottage? And why?

What made Jericho's walls come tumbling down?

And so on and on. Make up your own questions. It won't make any difference. The kids won't know what you're talking about. Thanks to our typical Sunday school, which goes all out for coloring books, paper dolls and gold stars on attendance charts instead of the great stories which are the mortar and the bricks of our Judaeo-Christian heritage.

For what it's worth, my own experience has been that

the Jews do better with their children in this respect than do most Christians.

But neither group does very well.

THE LAST NOEL
If things go on, 1984 ought just about to make
this sober fact . . .

P.S. 141 had done itself proud, everyone said.

Mr. Sangstrom's woodwinds had made the "Nutcracker Suite" come lushly alive, and the Elf Ballet from the combined third grades was glowing as much from the fond applause it had received from an admittedly partisan audience as from its vigorous performance of the "Skater's Waltz," complete with artificial blizzard.

Santa, in the padded person of principal Joe Quimby, had come and gone, scattering largess, painstakingly packaged by the P.T.A., among the less sophisticated primary pupils. He "ho-ho-ho'ed" magnificently, even though the effect was marred somewhat by an obbligato of subdued recognition on the part of the more knowledgeable fifth and sixth graders.

A rousing and concluding chorus of "Jingle Bells" had sent the small fry off to the cafeteria for cookies and punch served under the watchful and formidable eye of Mrs. Swenson, the food service director. The parents of P.S. 141 voted thanks to the faculty, voiced appreciation to the program committee and prepared to knock off for the holidays.

Thus it had been for Christmas after Christmas, back to

a time beyond which the memory of the oldest parent runneth not. But this once there was a brief hitch.

Old Mr. Chambers got to his feet from his vantage point on the aisle in the twelfth row of folding chairs. His granddaughter Elsie was third vice-president, and she had left the old man temporarily unattended while she went to round up some overlooked candy canes.

The cracked voice rang out querulously. "What happened to the carols?"

Everyone said later that it was the most embarrassing thing that had ever happened at a school Christmas party. Of course, old Chambers had lived on that Idaho ranch all his life until his wife died and he had come to the city where Elsie could take care of him, but just the same! Didn't the old fool know that carols had been proscribed from the schools since the late Sixties? Couldn't he realize that prayers, spoken or sung in any form, were now legally taboo?

Mrs. Grey, the flustered and mortified president, tried to explain as tactfully as possible. No use. Mr. Chambers was pretty excited.

"Can't have no Christmas without 'Silent Night' and 'Joy to the World'," he falsettoed. "So happens I've got my harmonica with me. I'll play 'em if you'll all sing."

And blessed if he didn't pull out a mouth organ and start in. Well, naturally this couldn't be allowed. Mrs. Grey was kind, but firm. She spoke for all the parents when she told Elsie's grandpa that no religious songs could be sung on the school grounds. The old man was incredulous.

"You mean they ain't singin' the Christmas songs no more? Why, in my day, everybody sang 'em and loved 'em. Regardless of religion. They're part of all of us. Who ever got hurt by a Christmas carol?"

Yes, sir. It was downright embarrassing. No one wanted to try to explain things to the red-faced, shouting old man. Finally they just all went home, after picking up the kids in the cafeteria, leaving a humiliated Elsie to try to get her grandpa to go home, too.

Grumbling, he went out into the parking lot at last, still clutching his harmonica. He shook off Elsie's arm and blew a defiant chorus of "O Come, All Ye Faithful." Luckily, everyone had gone, and no one heard it but his granddaughter.

For several minutes the old man stood quite still. Then he slipped the harmonica into his coat pocket and looked up searchingly into a frosty sky. Above the deep and dreamless sleep of all the city's children, it seemed that he and he alone could see the silent stars go by, and hear the angels sing.

Patriotism

Every state requires its schools to teach love of country.

And—at the risk of being called a square or even a cube —why not?

WHAT'S WRONG WITH LOVE?
Love, your magic spell is not quite everywhere . . .

The self-appointed Pied Pipers of today's youth have made a big thing out of hate. In dozens of espresso houses, on scores of windy campus quads, in umpteen hundred demonstrations they have been telling everyone who would listen that hate is what's wrong with the world: hate in Vietnam, hate in Alabama, hate among the right wingers. If we could just substitute big, warm, wonderful love for all this hate, they say, everything would be real cool.

Well, now, maybe they've got something. Of course, I'd like to be around, though at a safe distance, when our bearded and sandaled draft dodgers try selling the virtues of love as opposed to hate to those eminent peace lovers Ho Chi Minh and Mao Tse-tung. And I'm reasonably certain that the ghosts of the butchered Hungarian Freedom Fighters of a few years back would have a few things to say about the practical difficulty of loving Communist tank crews while they are busy crushing you to a jelly.

However, let us concede that these ofttimes slovenly striplings have a point. As the late Father Divine used to point out: "Peace, it's wonderful." And so is love, of course.

Which makes me wonder why, in all this talk about the positivism of love and the negativism of hate, no one ever seems to be concerned about love of country.

The official magazine of the Knights Templar recently discussed the results of two polls given to young Americans, one at the New York World's Fair and one among the Big Ten universities. In both, 84% of the students questioned denied the importance of patriotism and described it as unnecessary.

There were other interesting findings, too: 61% rejected the profit incentive; more than half were for government ownership of the nation's industries; 71% would deny an accused person the right to face his accuser.

Just as an aside to some of our creepier newspaper columnists and editorial writers who have been doing their best to create a congenial climate for this point of view, 41% of the kids favored canceling freedom of the press altogether. How do you like that one, fellows?

But it's the black eye hung on love which nonpluses me. That's all patriotism is, you know. Just love. And with all the blackguarding and downgrading of hate that's going on these days, I should have thought that hate's opposite —love—would begin to come into its own. Apparently not, or at least only in its more trivial manifestations, to be found in any pad.

Perhaps a clue can be found in the statement of a young teacher who recently declined to lead his students in saluting the American Flag. "The pledge mentions freedom and justice for all," he mused profoundly, "and I don't believe we have achieved freedom and justice in this country yet."

So we haven't attained perfect freedom yet. Your mother didn't give you perfect freedom either, did she? But does that prevent you from loving her?

Ideal justice is still somewhere in the dim future. Does your wife always treat you justly? And if, being human, she doesn't, are you going to quit telling her of your love for her? You'll have a fine, rewarding marriage, my friend. Just as you'll be a fine, rewarding citizen, I don't think.

It is good to seek after perfection. The very search cannot but ennoble those who take part in it. But to demand divine faultlessness as a prerequisite to love, or the public expression of that love, is to banish love from human affairs.

America is human, created by humans, populated by humans. As such, she will fall short of perfection from time to time. But with all her faults, she is still preeminently the fairest and the freest and the finest of all the countries of the world. She needs your love, and she needs to hear about it from you, even as your wife and mother do.

Why not tell her once in a while?

NO MORE SALUTING
Whatever happened to patriotic judges, anyhow?

"Hats on, the Flag is passing by!"

Apparently this is to be the marching slogan of our brave new world, at least if one West Coast court has its way. Recently a decision was handed down which freed school children from the bothersome obligation to salute their country's flag and to repeat the Pledge of Allegiance.

In the parlance of the day, it figures.

At about the same time, some of the creepier, just-out-from-under-a-rock types who infest the Berkeley campus of the University of California held a kind of beatnik version of the black mass in front of their local selective service headquarters, the ritual consisting of a public tearing-up of their draft cards. I must confess to a gentle glow of relief at the thought that these exalted exponents of existentialism would not be charged after all with the onerous responsibility of hemispheric defense. But I began to wonder just where it is all going to end.

Certainly if my son can now decline to salute the Colors merely because he decides he doesn't want to, he can also refuse to do certain other things for the same reason—things like bearing arms in his country's defense, paying his taxes to support policies he disapproves of or, for that matter, keeping his mouth shut in school so that the teacher can get the lesson taught.

The learned judge has opened a humdinger of a hornet's nest with this little juridical gem, much as old Justice Taney did a little more than a century ago when he decided that Dred Scott was forever a mere thing and chattel of his owner, wherever he might roam. Postscript: the American people decided differently. The court was overruled. As Lincoln remarked, "A judge is as apt to be right as any ordinary man, and no more so."

For the logical implication of this flag-salute decision is that every man—indeed every child—now is to be the sole arbiter of his own conduct. He is to be ruled only by his own conscience in his relation to organized society and to his fellow man, regardless of the wishes of the majority and the laws of the land.

Such a doctrine, if upheld, spells chaos for the nation and a death blow to the concept of responsible citizenship which harks back at least to Plato, which the schools are rightly charged with the duty of passing from one generation to the next.

The good citizen stands in relation to his country as the good son to his mother.

He obeys her because she is his elder, because she conjoins within herself the wisdom of many and because he owes to her his begetting and his nurturing.

He honors her above all others, placing her in a special niche within his secret heart, in front of which the candles of respect and admiration are forever kept alight.

He defends her against all enemies and counts his life well lost in her behalf.

Above all else he loves her, deeply and without display, knowing that although he shares that privilege with others the nature of his own affection is unique and personal, rising from the deepest wellsprings of his being—and it is returned in kind.

This is the good citizen. While his kind prevails, so also flourishes the Great Republic.

People rise to salute you, Your Honor, whenever you enter your courtroom, and rightly so. Is it too much to ask that a little of the same respect be taught to children as they rise in their places every morning to greet their country?

NINE DICTATORS ARE NO BETTER THAN A SINGLE TYRANT
*In fact, what ever happened to judges who had
brains enough to pound sand into a rat-hole?*

> "*The great object of my fear is the federal judiciary.
> That body, like gravity, ever acting with noiseless foot
> and alarming advance . . . is engulfing insidiously the
> special governments into the jaws of that which feeds
> them. It is a very dangerous doctrine to consider the
> judges as the ultimate arbiters of all constitutional matters.
> It is one which would place us under the despotism of an
> oligarchy.*"

JEFFERSON

Yes, boys and girls, it was old Tom who said this. Not
Barry Goldwater. Not even Robert Welch. It was Mr.
Democracy himself. And if this be treason, make the most
of it.

I wanted to point this out right off the bat, just in case
someone felt called upon to brand me a "Let's-Impeach-
Earl-Warren" member of the you-know-what. The author
of the Declaration of Independence, the third President of
these United States, the founder and patron saint of the
Democratic Party is, I hope, above such suspicion, even
in this murky era of guilt by association and rebuttal by
labeling.

What triggered the quotation from the Sage of Monti-
cello was the recent Supreme Court decision opening the
doors of New York classrooms to avowed Communists as
teachers and counselors. Justice Tom Clark in his scathing
minority opinion pointed out almost wistfully that his black-
robed brethren had, "by this broadside, swept away one of

our most precious rights—namely, the right of self-preservation."

It's true, you know.

When Uncle Sam goes, everything goes. The courts
which protect us. The schools which educate us. The
homes which nurture us.

As Justice Clark has said, the doors are open now. Open
to the tamperer, to the burglar, to the wild-eyed fanatic
with the torch. We seem to have the pretty dubious prospect of being the only great nation in all history to commit deliberate suicide.

But I guess this self-preservation stuff is stuffy and old-
fashioned nowadays. After all, how important is a nation's
right to defend itself as compared to a Communist's right
to subvert it?

Not very, according to the court majority. "Academic
freedom"—that's the important thing today, even though
there are as many definitions of this highly subjective
phrase as there are professors in our colleges. The high
court judges have formally given us that, in their own
words, they "will not tolerate laws which cast a pall of
orthodoxy over the classroom."

For "orthodoxy" read "patriotism." Or even "simple
decency."

O brave new world that hath such judges in it!

Make way now for Prof. Timothy Leary and his glassy-
eyed cult of LSD. And for the beatnik mouthers of the
Filthy Speech Movement. And for the Mafia and Murder,
Inc., for that matter. Nothing orthodox about THEM.

Why not?

Good manners are orthodox. So are virtuous morals. So

is clean speech. So is the ability to keep one's hands out of one's neighbor's pockets. If orthodoxy now casts a legal pall, it is not too farfetched to envision the classroom of the future as a cross betwen a Commie cell and a burlesque runway where nothing is banned.

If academic freedom is now more important than morality and love of country and sheer survival, then in its name literally anything goes. The lid is definitely off, and with it the traditional right of American parents ever since the founding of the Republic and long before to determine through their elected representatives just who should teach their children what.

Once, long ago, the Supreme Court in its arrogance trampled upon the conscience of the country. The Dred Scott decision legalized slavery in the North and presumably riveted it upon the nation for all time to come. Within a single decade, slavery was dead on this continent to the echo of great guns and to the outraged thunder of a betrayed and indignant populace.

So much for the infallibility of the court. Jefferson was right.

GROUP XI

People

All kinds of people.

Cops. Astronauts. Cartoonists. Actresses. Songwriters. Pilgrims. Even Santa Claus.

All of them play a part in education.

THE ASTRONAUTS: ANSWER
TO A BASIC AMERICAN NEED
*This one was written before several heroes gave
their lives for their country while using old
Earth as a launching pad into the Unknown.
It is published now in memoriam . . .*

Every once in a while a newspaper cartoon hits the exact
spot and points up a national mood or sentiment a thousand
times better than all the brilliant journalese which can be
brought to bear.

Tom Nast summed up the ponderosity of the Repub-
licans, the stubbornness of the Democrats and the predatory
ferocity of Tammany Hall in his trivial but telling take-
offs on the elephant, the donkey and the tiger. In so doing,
and quite incidentally, he sent Boss Tweed to jail, shook
up New York as it has not been shaken up since and carved
an enduring niche for himself in the reformers' hall of fame.

"Ding" Darling capped a lifetime of brilliant drawing
with his touching and gallant farewell to Teddy Roosevelt
the day after the great Rough Rider had voiced his last
"Bully!" His sketch of Roosevelt on a plunging stallion,
teeth and glasses all agleam, following the last Conestoga

wagons into the sunset and waving the rest of us on with a flourish of his ten-gallon hat, summed up Roosevelt better than all the biographies before or since. It may just be the greatest cartoon ever drawn.

But the craft is far from dead. Just a short time ago, when the marvelous Mariner was winging its way past Mars and sending back those unbelievable pictures of the red planet, a cartoon appeared in my morning paper which bore the authentic stamp of genius. The Mariner, surrounded by the blackness of interplanetary space, was portrayed with the hull and rigging of an ancient, ghostly galleon. From one world to another she floated like thistledown, and beneath her was Coleridge's titanic line about another haunted voyager:

> "We were the first who ever burst
> Into that silent sea . . ."

Could anything be finer or more expressive of the basic American need "to strive, to seek, to find and not to yield"?

And this leads me in due course to those direct descendants of Odysseus and Marco Polo, Kit Carson and John C. Fremont: the astronauts. Above and beyond all their explorings and adventurings, their gifts to theoretical science and their journeyings to uncharted lands is their unique value as examples to our children. For my money, nothing else they may do will be half so important as their effect on the kids.

Every generation of children has its heroes. Medieval youngsters steeped themselves in the lore of King Arthur and Sir Lancelot. Merrie England rang with the deeds of Robin Hood. French youth thrilled to the song of Roland

and his paladins. Our own grandsires read Ned Buntline wide-eyed and breathlessly and made folk-heroes out of Buffalo Bill and Wild Bill Hickok.

And this is profoundly good and right. Each generation grown to manhood and womanhood is conditioned willy-nilly by the ideals and attitudes of the heroes whom it worshiped in childhood. There is a deep-seated, fundamental need involved here, every bit as basic as the need for food or security or love.

For a while I was afraid we'd be turning over America's reins in a few years to a new breed whose heroes had been Mario Savio and the Beatles. But the exploits of Glenn, Schirra and those who have followed them out into space have assured us of 20th century idols not one whit inferior to Jason's Argonauts and Arthur's Table Round.

And not a day too soon. In a world where phoniness is a way of life and cynical debauchery a built-in feature of the current scene, the clear-eyed, unassuming, steel-nerved astronauts come as a desperately needed answer to an educator's prayer. At last we have someone alive and real and essentially decent to hold up to the small fry as stuff of which heroes are made. Best of all, they look the part. And—unexpected manna from a reluctant heaven!—every single one of them is an educated man, and proud of it.

Not the least of their appeal to youth, paradoxically enough, is the essential *impracticality* of what they are doing. All the ancient heroes practiced heroism for its own sake, not to cement themselves with the "in" group or to make a fast buck. I think we are about due as a nation for a healthy backlash against the cult of the cool and the Great Society of gray-flanneled facelessness.

Forget what we may find on the moon. It's the getting there that counts. That and the vicarious redemption of a whole generation from the coils of apathy, inertia and noninvolvement.

For when the new heroes blast off from Cape Kennedy on their chargers of steel and flame, they carry with them millions of our children, eyes shining with a new and otherworldly vision, lifted if only for a moment from the mess we've made of things. Riders to the stars.

A GOOD WORD FOR THE FIRST THANKSGIVERS
How easy it is now to sneer at the breaking
waves dashing high on the stern and
rockbound coast. How many of us could
have licked what they licked?

Every November, when I was a boy, the Pilgrim Fathers would be unveiled to me in school as gray-clad saints with buckles on their hats and shoes. As W.S. Gilbert once remarked about someone else, they went around uttering "platitudes in stained-glass attitudes."

My teachers nonetheless managed to impress me with the really significant things about these somewhat formidable ancestors: their faith, their dogged courage, their determination to adjust their hostile environment to themselves.

Then, about a generation ago, came the debunkers with burning eyes fastened unwaveringly upon the fast buck. Nobody was spared. Daniel Webster turned out to be a gabby alcoholic. Paul Revere? Actually yellow to the core.

Washington was a profane old slave-owner. Ben Franklin was a sly libertine.

But the choicest target of the debunkers was the Plymouth Rock legend. Evarts sneered that the pilgrims "fell first upon their own knees and then upon the aborigines." Elder Brewster and Gov. Bradford were called everything from pious frauds to ranting fanatics.

The Pilgrims, it seems were not heroic at all. They hanged witches. They dunked gossipy housewives in the village pond. They made everybody go to church, and they rapped Sabbath sleepyheads on the sconce with long-handled doorknobs.

All these things, incidentally, are perfectly true. Taken out of historical context thus, they project an image of blue-nosed bigotry calculated to inspire in the student of today's "new history" the same pride in his ancestry that he would feel in descending from Bloody Mary, Torquemada or Hermann Goering.

But what kind of image would we project to our great-grandchildren, I wonder, if the scholars of the year 2000 told them that we spent our time ingesting LSD, rioting in the streets, parading in Ku Klux bedsheets and exploding H-bombs? And all these things are true, too, to a certain extent.

You cannot judge 20th century America by the standards of the 21st century. Neither can we call 17th century Americans to purse-lipped account because they failed to live up to some of the alleged ideals and ethics of today.

Certainly our ancestors—the Puritans, incidentally, not the Pilgrims—put witches to death. So did just about every-

body else in the 1600s. The big difference lay in the fact
that the rest of the world barbecued the old ladies over slow
fires on sunny afternoons while our Massachusetts forebears humanely hanged them.

And if Miles Standish and his men did chivy the hapless
aborigines a mite too much, it was tea and crumpets compared to what the Spaniards were doing to the Caribs, the
Dutch to the Hottentots, and the Russians to practically
everybody they could get their hands on.

No, the storm-tossed, hunger-racked Mayflower passengers deserve something better at our hands than cheap
jokes and lofty disapproval from our comfortable vantage
point of historical hindsight.

They hit a beach that raw December day as strange as
Mars will be to us. No trim, primrosed New England
gardens smiled a welcome to them nor quaintly cobbled
streets nor yet white clapboard churches with gabled bel-
fries and spires pointing like fingers at the steely northern
sky. All these lay somewhere on ahead, to be fought for
and wept over and wrested atom by atom, stone by painful
stone from a reluctant future.

Half of them died that first hellish year. Frozen. Fevered.
Starved. Scurvied.

The survivors took root. Not all the bitter winds that
blew could roust them from the rocky soil and piney hills
of old New England. A century and a half later their
stubborn, dour descendants looked down British muskets
at Lexington and Concord, died beneath a new flag at
Saratoga and Yorktown and in God's time made us a
nation.

What cause for thanks had they that first November on

a savage continent? Their freedom and their faith. Nothing more.

And how stands our treasure-house of blessings today as the golden time of gratitude rolls around? Full to bursting. Overflowing. Thanks still to freedom and to faith and to a few grim men and their uncomplaining women in funny hats and buckled shoes so long ago.

Remember them Thanksgiving Day. They planted us here.

HALT! WHO GOES THERE?
It's because he's the Spirit of Christmas, I guess.
Spirits aren't very welcome in our brave new
world. Unless they're bottled, of course . . .

My state has a nice, toothy, antiloitering law which prevents idlers, dope peddlers and other undesirables from lounging around school premises and annoying the kids. I used it the other day to give the bum's rush to an odd old character who was trying to get inside the school grounds with a sleigh full of suspicious-looking commodities.

"Name?" I asked suspiciously.

"Just call me Chris," he beamed through his whiskers.

"What's in the bag, Chris?" I probed.

"Glad you asked," the old fellow ho-ho-hoed, and he dumped the whole mess out onto the sidewalk. I had visions of a protest strike by our overworked custodians, but I persevered in the politest tradition of my profession.

"Identify each article, please."

Chris sat right down on the school walk, getting some black hop-scotch chalk on his bright red pants in the process.

"First a manger scene complete with donkeys and sheep," he said happily. "Some of the big-city youngsters have never seen either one."

"Sorry," I replied frostily. "A creche is a symbol of aggressive Christian sectarianism, and the Supreme Court takes a pretty dim view of that, in case you hadn't heard."

Our uninvited guest seemed a bit taken aback.

"How about some shining scarlet candles and some tinkling silver bells?"

Completely unthinkable, of course. Candles are a part of Jewish ritual, and bells were used by Ikhnaton and his Egyptian sun-worshipers to welcome old Ra every morning. I told Chris so. I told him, too, that if he persisted in trying to sneak religious objects into a public school he was going to be in serious trouble.

"But this is ridic—. Never mind!" he blurted, digging into his bag a little deeper. "Here's a nice Christmas tree, all decorated for the kiddies to look at and admire."

I was beginning to be shocked.

"A Christmas tree! Are you asking me to let you in here with that living example of the Germanic Odin-cult, and probably a phallic symbol to boot?"

The little old trespasser got up slowly, dusting off his baggy trousers. His eyes no longer twinkled.

"I suppose holly and mistletoe are out of the question?"

"Holly and mistletoe? Are you trying to proselytize Druidism in a tax-supported institution? Celtic paganism is just as forbidden as any other kind of religion, you know."

Chris looked at me humbly.

"No, I didn't know. I always used to be welcome everywhere. Wherever the children gathered at the happy, glowing, golden time of year when the nights are longest and the need of the little ones for love and joy and wonder is greatest. Things *have* changed, haven't they?"

"They certainly have," I answered firmly. "If our courts have their way there's going to be no such thing as Christmas in the schools. Or Hanukah. Or Ramadan, for that matter."

Chris sagged a little and began to repack his bag.

"How strange," he muttered to himself. "When life today has so little joy at best, how sad to take that little away from the children."

I bristled.

"You'd better take all that propaganda and get out of here," I warned him.

"I will," he assured me. And that's when it happened. He started humming "God Rest Ye Merry, Gentlemen" as he got into his sleigh, and some of the school children heard him through an open classroom window.

No use dwelling on what happened next. I called the cops, of course. Chris is in jail downtown, and his reindeer are being cared for by the local SPCA. He won't be back. The separation of church and state has been maintained. The children are safe.

I guess my only question is this:

When I inspected the silent, sterile, rigidly functional school building that night before I locked up and went home, why did I shiver—hard?

All the thermostats were working fine.

OFFICER CLANCY: GUARDIAN OF THE RAINBOW BRIDGE
*If I were a policeman today, I'm afraid I'd hate
everybody. Fortunately, I'm not—and the
policeman doesn't . . .*

> " 'Confound Romance.' . . . and all unseen
> Romance brought up the nine-fifteen."

> KIPLING

It isn't dead. It's just changed, like the rest of us.

Oh, I know. We've killed some of its faithful allies. Chivalry and modesty and piety are breathing their last, cut off by the computers, put to the sword by the pragmatists, slain by the Sick Sixties. But somehow Romance survives.

Not like the lambent lovers' moon—Shakespeare's silver bow new-bent in heaven—Shelley's orbed maiden with white fire laden—beneath whose calm, incurious countenance our thewed and squat progenitors sang at the mouths of caves the oldest of all songs to the long-haired Eves who crouched so cautiously within. This moon we've killed and left its pale corpse a pile of slag and gray rock to circle us endlessly in a sky littered with metallic junk.

Not like the human heart, which chilled for Stevenson and burned for Scott, which leaped and fainted and was bruised and broken in uncounted sonnets written by a million-million lovesick swains. We've done what the sonneteers could never do in all the ages past and gone. We've shattered the human heart for good and all and planted in its place a fist-size package of reflex muscle imminently exchangeable with sterile plastic and with shining steel.

But Romance thus far defies us. I hope it always will.

Webster defines it in part as "a disposition to delight in the heroic, the adventurous, the mysterious." Romance is all of that, and more. It's living dangerously. It's championing lost causes. It's fighting for the right and protecting the weak and defying overwhelming odds. It's willingness to die for duty's sake.

"A nice thought," I hear you murmuring wistfully, "but where are we to find in this society of noninvolvement and unfeelingness a practitioner of this philosophy?"

Just look around. You see him every day. He's generally in blue or khaki, and he's usually the last fellow you want to see.

He's a cop. A plain, flat-footed, somewhat rueful policeman.

Now don't tell me he's sometimes rude, occasionally brutal and once in a while bigoted. Of course he is. So are some schoolteachers and some insurance salesmen and even some congressmen. He has problems with his wife and owes money and worries about his kids. Just like all of us.

Because, you see, he *is* one of us. With one added, all-important dimension. He puts his life on the line for the rest of us.

Sure, he gets paid for it. But there's more to the law enforcement man than just a pay check. He stands between us and unimaginable brutality, lust and sadism. He is abused more savagely than any other professional. He is ridiculed. It's always open season on the cops. And recently our courts have indeed made it necessary for him to defy overwhelming odds.

He is one of the last of the true romantics, even if he may not look much like one.

The old Norsemen had a warrior god named Heimdall who guarded the Rainbow Bridge between heaven and earth. He could hear grass growing in the fields and wool on the backs of sheep. Everything that happened among warring, bickering humanity he watched and noted and reported to great Odin. He carried a mighty trumpet like Gabriel's, with which to arouse the gods when evil and crime had overwhelmed the world and threatened to march on heaven itself.

Our blue and khaki Heimdalls today are blowing horns, in the guise of whistles, even as the tide of violence ebbs and flows in our very streets. They stand grimly at bay, and the Rainbow Bridge between the criminal and ourselves shudders and totters beneath their feet. And in our own suburban versions of Valhalla we snore comfortably in our beds, heedless of Heimdall's horn, content in the ancient knowledge that Heimdall guards the gates.

When Ragnarok came at last—the Twilight of the Gods —the great defender fought uncomplainingly to the end and slew at last the wicked Spirit of Evil, falling himself in the moment of triumph. But by this time, civilization was dead and humanity decimated.

I grow old. Wind and muscle run to seed. But what I can do, I will—to give a little help to Heimdall before the bridge goes down.

GALBRAITH'S INTERESTING IMAGE OF HIGHER EDUCATION
*An example of how one well-meaning egghead
can wreck whole institutions . . .*

All of us in the school business can rest more easily now that Harvard's John Kenneth Galbraith has solved the problems of American higher education in one fell swoop. As quoted in a recent official communique, the Bernard Baruch of the In-Group Jet Set solemnly informed a presumably palpitating public that the way to cure our current collegiate chaos is to let the professors take over and run things.

As one member of the embattled University of California's board of regents who recently watched several hundred professors there lie down and play Philistines to Mario Savio's decidedly unbarbered Samson, I developed certain strong reservations about the managerial and administrative skills of those particular cap-and-gowned temporizers with violence.

But let Prof. Galbraith speak for himself:

"Poor universities composed of craven men are invariably very orderly places, and bad universities have the silence and tranquility of the desert."

and

"No one is so silly as to suppose that there is such a thing as orderly, well-regulated debate which can be carefully tailored in advance to the taste of the audience."

and finally

"I have no doubt the modern (university) governing board has a certain ceremonial role. Possibly it can best be converted to an instrument of faculty administration by having faculties elect a suitable majority of members to it."

Note Prof. Galbraith's three blithe assumptions:

1—That orderliness and dignity and scholarly decorum are manifestations of cowardice, and quiet contemplation is relegated to the Sahara.

This is the boiler-factory concept of higher learning. It substitutes shouting and parading for thinking and is just what the doctor ordered for the hulking, hairy minority of students who boast muscles stronger than mentalities.

2—That debate about the great issues of our time is automatically suspect if it is conducted according to any accepted rules of procedure.

This is the adrenal theory of the university, sometimes known as the nut-house hypothesis. It would have fascinated such pre-Galbraithian mossbacks as Socrates, St. Thomas Aquinas and Immanuel Kant, all of whom managed somehow to conduct their earth-shaking probes into the nature of the universe within the accepted framework of orderly logic and debate. And without booing, spitting or going limp, I may add.

3—That a democratically founded and financed public institution should be turned over to its inmates, lock, stock and barrel.

A tiny intellectual elite, representing no constituency on God's earth except itself, should be allowed to spend millions of public tax dollars as it alone sees fit, and throughout this academic safari with other people's money the elite should be answerable to absolutely nobody. This, I regret to say, is the fascist postulate in regard to the governance of any public entity, from the Nuremberg city council to the University of California. And the sooner all of us recognize it for what it is, the better.

Prof. Galbraith is unquestionably a learned authority on subjects ranging from how to perpetuate the permanent welfare state to how to survive a Kennedy cocktail party without being pushed into a swimming pool. But heaven forfend that he should be encouraged in his current development of a metaphysics justifying the reduction of our great college campuses to a lowest common denominator consisting of LSD, four-letter words and policeman-biting.

Higher education exists to pursue the truth and to provide young people with the intellectual tools they need to conduct a lifelong and even-handed search after that highly elusive commodity.

But it does not exist to breed booers, blusterers and bully-boys. And if this makes me a craven in your book, Professor, I guess I'll just have to confess that quite a number of things frighten me these days.

Including you.

BEING A PROPHET CAN BE PRETTY FRUSTRATING
It's tough to be a schoolman these days . . .

A friend of mine got fired some time ago. His name is Carl Hansen and, until the ax which seemingly hangs above all school superintendents these days fell on him, he was in charge of the schools in Washington, D.C.

Technically, I guess Carl wasn't fired. He "resigned"

right after a federal judge outlawed the "track" system of pupil ability grouping which Carl had pioneered in the Washington schools.

Reason: The judge held that this instructional technique discriminated against pupils who happened to come from low socio-economic groups.

Result: Carl's justly famous "Amidon Plan" went down the drain, and Carl decided he might as well bow out, too.

This sort of thing is precisely comparable to some pompous jurist ruling out one particular kind of brain surgery in the Mayo Clinic on the grounds that all brains are alike and, therefore, all brain operations should be identical.

I have never met Carl Hansen, but that does not alter the fact that he is a friend of mine. He's also a friend of every school man and woman and school child in these United States. Most especially he's a friend of the Negro youngsters, whom he knows and understands better than almost any other educator in the land.

He introduced more worthwhile innovations and did more original thinking while in Washington than did any other 10 superintendents of schools I can think of offhand. He almost literally knocked himself out trying to prove that a school district which is 90% black can do just as good a job with its children as can a district which is 90% white.

The thanks he got was a kick in the teeth.

The thing that gets my goat—hoofs, horns and whiskers —is the blithely infuriating assumption currently being made by so many judges that all you have to do is to mix a school population with a racial eggbeater and hey! presto, you will automatically get a good educational cake.

It is not that simple, your honor. I wish it were. It would have been a lot better for the Washington children, as a matter of fact, if you had come right out and admitted that you know as little about education as I know about jurisprudence, and that, therefore, you were not going to assume a highly technical competence which in fact you do not possess.

I'll even make a deal with you, judge. You stop meddling with our classrooms and I'll guarantee that we teachers won't interfere with the way you run your courtroom.

Almost 10 years ago, I wrote the following in *Suffer, Little Children*: "It is already possible to trace the path of the racial whirlwind by the strewn professional corpses of educators."

There is little satisfaction in being proved accurate on such a sad prophecy as this one. Within the last year or so, Ben Willis "retired" under fire in Chicago. Harold Spears did the same in San Francisco. Cal Gross got the sack in New York. Then it was Carl Hansen's turn. In each case, a man who had devoted his entire life to the service of children left a job which desperately needed him because he had "failed" to solve a problem which nobody else in the country has been able even to half-solve.

The so-called "track" system simply puts children of like abilities together for parts of the school day so that they can learn at the same rate using materials of comparable difficulty. It has nothing to do with race, color, creed, wealth, poverty or what Dad thinks of the man in the White House.

In some schools it works fine. In others it bombs out. But this is true of just about everything in education. It depends upon time and circumstance and above all upon who does the teaching.

One thing, though, I'm reasonably sure of: we teachers don't need any judges to point out our mistakes. Lord knows they make enough of their own these days.

THE LAND BEYOND THE RAINBOW
The happy blending of author and child-mind. It
happened once before, with a shy mathematician
and a long-haired little girl in Victoria's England.
By the grace of a God who loves little children,
it happened yet again, in our own time . . .

There is an old dispute among educators as to who was the greatest writer of children's books. Lewis Carroll was probably the most imaginative and whimsical. Robert Louis Stevenson was far and away the best stylist. Such literary titans as Defoe and Swift don't count, inasmuch as *Robinson Crusoe* and *Gulliver* were never intended originally for the child audience. Kipling's *Just-So-Stories* and *Jungle Book* fascinate adults more than they do the small fry.

No, the palm belongs to a little man whose style was primitive, his humor labored, his "message" nonexistent. Yet he sold more books to children than did all the giants in the first paragraph put together.

His name was L. Frank Baum, and he invented Oz.

It was quite a counry, too. Neatly divided among the Munchkins, Winkies, Quadlings and Gillikins, it had an Emerald City as its capital and was cut off from our more conventional time and space by the burning sands of the

Dreadful Desert. Its inhabitants put Carroll's Wonderland denizens to shame. There were not only witches, but sorceresses, wizards and fairy princesses to boot, to say nothing of gnomes, live sawhorses and woggle-bugs.

Baum wrote dozens of Oz books, and they sold like hotcakes. His plots were invariable: children roaming picaresquely through an enchanted countryside, confronting strange creatures, befriended by talking animals, safeguarded in the end by a beneficent and all-powerful White Magic. The formula was as old as Aesop, as wistfully appealing as Hans Christian Andersen, as durable as the Brothers Grimm.

I was sharply reminded of little Mr. Baum recently when for the umpteenth time I watched his classic *Wizard of Oz*, this time on color television. Forty years fell suddenly away, and I was back in my mother's kitchen, perched on a high stool, breathlessly and stumblingly reading to her the chapter about the flying monkeys so that she, too, would know the wonder and the excitement of the discovery I had made.

Children all over America were doing that, I suppose. And there was a reason. Baum plumbed unconsciously the very depths of the child soul. Dorothy from Kansas was any child from anywhere. The Scarecrow seeking wisdom personified our curiosity about life and the universe. The Tin Woodman looked for a heart, and we children sought love and affection right along with him. The Cowardly Lion symbolized the secret fears which haunt every childhood—a time, incidentally, not quite so happy and carefree as grownups would like to remember it.

I thought of all this as I watched the old film. And what

an evergreen, joyous combination of adventure and spectacle and fun it is, to be sure. Its colors are as fresh, its songs as lilting, its cast as winning as when it was made almost three decades ago.

Hollywood has had much to answer for since those halcyon days, but when it put together the best of its talents and its techniques to make *Wizard*, it laid up compensating crowns in heaven for itself. If only it would use its genius today to keep us young at heart instead of pandering to the oldest, the shabbiest, the shoddiest parts of each of us!

One final thought. *Wizard's* little star, Judy Garland, has grown older and graver, like all of us who watched her skipping down the yellow brick road with those three amiable companions so long ago. She may have long since wearied of that simple, sad little song about the rainbow, though she still sings it as graciously and beautifully as ever.

It is not easy to be the center of a classic, to become in a very real sense immortal when one is still a child. It haunts you down the years. Everything you try to do is measured against that one supreme and magic moment when all the stars were right and nothing you could do was wrong.

Moments like that come seldom, if ever, to us ordinary mortals. When they come to a child and then pass on, never to return, they may create such problems for that child grown to womanhood as few of us have ever had to face.

And yet all of us are seen through a glass darkly, never as we really are. I think there may be harder fates than skipping down the winding road of time, arm in arm with

Love and Wisdom and Kindness, forever young, forever welcomed by the laughing hearts and the bright eyes of childhood.

Only one of all our millions, Judy, could bring our greatest fairy tale to everlasting life. There are far worse things than being Dorothy.

THE MAN WHO WROTE AMERICA'S SONGS
An awesome phenomenon of the twentieth century—which I presume our grandchildren will begin to appreciate.

> *"Give me the making of a nation's songs, and I care not who makes its laws."*
>
>   FLETCHER

It was 9 in the morning, and I was listening in the doorway while a class of fourth graders started school with a rousing chorus of "God Bless America." Gallantly oblivious to the imminent Supreme Court thunders which might reverberate around their heroic little heads, the youngsters shrilly and happily urged the Deity to "stand beside her and guide her through the night with a light from above."

It wasn't Kate Smith by a long shot. Some of the kids were a little flat, and one or two were obviously racing to see which one could finish first. But as I listened, echoes of other songs from other years sung by singers from vastly different times hummed in my ears.

Al Jolson belting out "Mandy." Crosby crooning "White Christmas." Astaire singing and dancing to "Easter Parade."

Laughing ghosts in tin hats and puttees protesting "Oh, How I Hate to Get Up in the Morning," and their G.I. sons in olive drab and paratroop boots raising a wistful "I Left My Heart at the Stagedoor Canteen."

As the children sang another chorus, the Roaring Twenties came and stood beside me, complete with raccoon coat and pennant, whispering "Blue Skies," "All Alone" and "Say It With Music." The Starving Thirties were there with "Let's Have Another Cup of Coffee," and the Fighting Forties marched in to the rhythm of "This Is the Army."

Yes, the piping little soprano voices, male and female, rang all these melodic changes on the carillon of memory for me, and for a moment I wondered why. Then I remembered. All these songs, and many more of equal note, had been written by one man. And what a man.

He is still very much with us today: a smallish, spry, bright-eyed fellow who rarely makes the news because he's always been decent, law-abiding and a quiet lover of his country who prefers not to make a big thing out of it.

His name, of course, is Irving Berlin. He has written more hit songs than any other man who ever lived. He has operated at full steam over a longer period of time than any other composer in history, starting in 1907 and still going strong. In his own highly competitive field he's the all-time champ and a full-blown, star-spangled genius.

If there be indeed such a thing as a musical mirror of 20th century America, this lilting little transplant from the steppes of Czarist Russia made it, owns it and has been holding it up to all the rest of us for more than 60 years. From "Alexander's Ragtime Band" a half-century ago to

"Empty Pockets" just the other day, a veritable cascade of Americana in music has flowed from this miraculous human cornucopia of song.

He grew up on the same dirty, brawling, warm-hearted East Side as Winchell and Jessel, Cantor and Jolson. Truly there must have been something in the very air of little old New York back around the turn of the century which quickened the hearts and brightened the voices of these Jewish children whose parents had brought them so far and at such cost in search of freedom.

Whatever it was, it made them great and famous and beloved. More importantly, it made them Americans, as only those who have fought and starved to reach these shores can be Americans.

Through all the countless Berlin tunes which poured from that battered little piano with the funny keyboard into the homes and the hearts of so many millions there breathed always a genuine if simple sentiment, a respect for womanhood which heartbreakingly seems so quaint to us today and, more than anything else, an all-encompassing love of his adopted country.

It is not given to every man to write a second national anthem nor to live on through all the years ahead on the lips and in the voices of America's children.

God bless America. And God bless Irving Berlin.

AL CAPP: THE DIOGENES OF DOGPATCH
Truth occasionally wears motley . . .

I'm so old I can remember when comic strips used to be comical.

I can remember Andy Gump, whose chin was conspicuous by its total absence and whose anguished cry of "Oh, Min!" convulsed a whole generation of newspaper readers over their morning coffee.

Then there were the Katzenjammer Kids, Hans und Fritz, who were jolly juvenile delinquents long before there was such a term and who inflicted upon the hapless Captain and Der Inspector torments unknown since the days of Torquemada.

Incredible as it may seem, my memory goes clear back to Happy Hooligan and his pillbox hat and lingers fondly on the Toonerville Trolley's gallery of grotesques, which included Mickey (Himself) McGuire and Aunt Eppie Hogg, the Fattest Woman in Three Counties.

Today's alleged "comics" bear the same relationship to those of my childhood as Boris Karloff bears to Charlie Chaplin. Little Orphan Annie undergoes daily disasters so dire that they have permanently stunted her growth. Dick Tracy has characters who laser-beam each other and French-fry their foes in boiling oil. Even Gordo turned into a were-cat recently, with a face guaranteed to frighten myriads of moppets right out of their rompers.

And so it goes. If the comic strips truly mirror our national frustrations and our collective state of mind, as certain psychologists maintain, then we are indeed in one heck of a shape.

There is one shining exception to all this. No horrors. No lachrymose tragedy. Not even serialized soap opera. Just slapstick comedy punctuated by homespun dialogue-cum-dialect and designed to hold up to healthy hilarity the frantic foibles of our so-called civilization.

I'm referring, of course, to Al Capp's *Li'l Abner*. For almost a generation the amiable hillbilly has been one of the few bright spots in my morning paper. I can laugh at Pappy Yokum and Marryin' Sam when I'm ready to burst into tears over just about everything else in the confounded sheet. And while Capp's humor is certainly broad, it is uniformly sane.

There is another dimension to Li'l Abner, however, which makes it a 20th century counterpart of the medieval morality play and which harks back even farther to the old Roman pantomimes. That is the ability of its creator to satirize on a grand scale without descending to personal invective and to accomplish this by creating living embodiments of national quirks and crotchets in a manner unknown since the late Charles Dickens.

Thus, American big business is preserved for posterity, like a fly in amber, in the muscled and mustachioed person of General Bullmoose, who believes with all his hard old devious heart that what's good for Bullmoose is good for the country. The edible shmoos and their cousins the kickable kygmies showed us devastatingly what happens to a nation when it suddenly gets everything it wants.

More recently it was the Students Wildly Indignant

About Nearly Everything. Actually, these burning-eyed S.W.I.N.E. were not caricatures at all. I have personally watched S.W.I.N.E. under another set of initials demonstrating on one of our college campuses and featuring paraders whose matted hairiness and over-all destructiveness made Capp's cartooned characters look by comparison like Herbert Hoover and his Cabinet. But the Capp take-offs linger long in the mind, don't they?

Yes, I suspect that in this pint-sized, peppery cartoonist we have an authentic, home-grown genius. His Abner is America itself—big, smiling, patriotic, decent, lovable, a little stupid. His Dogpatch, rickety though it is, shimmers green and gold and gladsome, as America did, once, before we set to work to ruin and pollute it in our own time.

His heroes are honorable and loyal and clean, thus, well-nigh unique these days.

Al Capp gets his message across to more people every day than any educator in the land. I've known educators with a lot worse message, too.

Welcome to the club, Al. If Aristophanes were alive today, I think he might be drawing Li'l Abner.

THE MAN WHO BUCKED THE TREND

> *If he earns your praise, bestow it; if you like him let him*
>   *know it;*
> *Let the words of true encouragement be said;*
> *Do not wait till life is over and he's underneath the*
>   *clover,*
> *For he cannot read his tombstone when he's dead.*

BRALEY

He was a friend of mine, as indeed he was a friend
of all mankind. I wrote this and he read it when
he alone knew he was dying. Thank God my
timing was right for a change . . .

We educators are a close-knit clan, proud of our pedagogy, devoted to our degrees, covetous of our credentials. Outsiders like Admiral Rickover who come nosing around our hunting preserves usually get the kind of treatment reserved for an umpire at a South American soccer match. The admiral, fortunately, is tough and doesn't care, but it's pretty rugged on the average fellow we find trespassing on our premises.

There is one shining, tremendous exception to this rule. He is a quiet fellow with no great shucks of a formal education, as I recall. He didn't write any books that I have heard of. He was never a college president or a professor or even a state superintendent of schools. Yet he ranks as the greatest educator of this century—greater than John Dewey or James Conant or all the rest of us put together.

His name is Walt Disney, and he operates out of Hollywood, of all places.

Like a lot of people, he came up once, long ago, with a gimmick. It was a highly unlikely mouse with a twisted grin and a squeaking falsetto which was Walt's very own. It made him, and it was followed by other gimmicks: an irascible duck, a dopey dog and a cow named Clarabell. The money rolled in. This would have been enough for most of us.

Not for Walt. The gimmicks gave him the wherewithal to build a springboard from which he launched into something unprecedented on this or any other continent—compensatory education for a whole generation of America's children. The classics written by the towering geniuses out of the past who had loved children enough to write immortal stories for them began to live and breathe again in the midst of a cynical, sin-seeking society which had allowed them to pass almost completely into the limbo of the forgotten.

Before the enchanted ken of the little ones Pinnochio danced once more on unsteady wooden legs. Snow White fled the witch's envy. Little Alice talked with rabbits and went into a land which only children can really understand. And most like Walt himself, of course, there was that boy who never grew up, who never lost the wonder and the glamor of childhood, Peter Pan.

His live movies have become lone sanctuaries of decency and health in the jungle of sex and sadism created by the Hollywood producers of pornography. Walt's pictures don't dwell on dirt. They show life as something a little finer than drunken wallowing in some gutter of self-pity. The beatniks and degenerates think his films are square.

I think they're wonderful.

One of his recent ones, they say, will make a pretty penny—Academy Awards and all that. I hope it makes $100 million. It's about time, for all our sakes, that a picture like this came along and cleaned up, in more ways than one.

Many, many years from now—decades, I hope—when this magical Pied Piper of our time wanders out of this imperfect world which he has done so much to brighten and adorn, millions of laughing, shouting little ghosts will follow in his train—the children that you and I once were, so long ago, when first a gentle magician showed us Wonderland.

GROUP XII

Teachers

Mine own people . . .

A TEACHER'S PRIVATE LIFE
We don't have to be as faultless as Caesar's wife.
But we should be a little better than Caesar's
mistress . . .

We're hearing increasingly these days that a teacher should never be called to account for what he does or says on his own time.

"After all," runs the argument, "a teacher is an American citizen. His spare time is his own. As long as he doesn't commit a jailable crime when he's off duty, whose business is it what he does away from his pupils?"

I'll tell you whose business it is. It's mine. It's yours. It's every parent's business, and very much so.

Why? Because we don't just hire a teacher to give lectures and assign homework and grade tests and filter facts into the skulls of his students. A teacher is also supposed to be an example to the small fry, to be the kind of gentleman we hope our boys will emulate or the kind of lady we would like our girls to become. And this particular portion of the job specifications pretty well rules out the drunken teacher, the immoral teacher, the profane or foul-mouthed or blasphemous teacher.

Whether he is lying in a gutter in front of the school or down the street a few blocks, whether he is seducing a pupil in class or taking her home with him, whether he is writing dirty poetry on the classroom blackboard or authoring a filthy play to be produced in the local little theater, has mighty little to do with the obvious fact that he's in the wrong business and should be chucked out of it as soon as possible.

It is not when or where a teacher does something improper that makes him unfit to be around children; it is the "something" itself which rules him out. The geography of iniquity, the chronology of turpitude are gloriously irrelevant to the main issue, which is the fact of the sin itself.

Children are little pitchers with big ears. When something Teacher has done goes sour, they—unlike the legendary betrayed husband—are usually the first to know. And since kids tend to identify very closely with their teachers, the implications are obvious and so serious that every civilization in the history of the planet has demanded higher standards of ethics and conduct on the part of its instructors than it has from its statesmen and its savants, its doctors and its ditch-diggers—higher standards indeed than from any other occupational group except its priests and holy men.

Today's American teacher, by and large, lives up to the traditions of his great profession. He is perhaps a freer man than was his predecessor insofar as his personal habits are concerned. In most places now, an occasional cocktail or cigarette won't entail his professional ruin. He may entertain pretty much as he likes, and his churchgoing—or lack of it—is more and more considered to be his own business.

All this is good. Teachers aren't saints, nor should they be expected to be. But they are expected to live soberly and decently, to avoid public scandal for the sake of their wide-eyed daily charges and above all to set an example in their speech, their actions and their writings which will be an inspiration to the next generation, not an emetic.

Recently a teacher's credential was called into question because of a piece of alleged literature she had written in her spare time. It was studded with epithets and outhouse prose which none of the newspapers which sprang so ardently to her defense would have dared for one moment to reprint.

The state committee which eventually studied the case and incidentally took no action against her was criticized in unbridled terms for even daring to question her excursion into the realm of public scatology. You would have thought the committee had commited some crime.

"I suppose Shakespeare himself would have been unable to qualify as a teacher in your state," sneered one of the letters which blizzarded in from the bleeding hearts.

As a matter of fact, old Will would have been denied his credential. As I recall, he was convicted of deer-stealing once upon a time, which in my state is grand theft and a disqualifying felony.

So what?

Shakespeare was a towering genius, but he never claimed to be a teacher. So was Lord Byron, who practiced whole-sale adultery and occasional incest. So was Francois Villon, who snatched purses for a living. So was Kit Marlowe, who lived and died in a brothel. We are the richer for the literary legacy left by these but we wouldn't let Byron, Villon or Marlowe come within a city block of our children.

Genius may qualify a man to go down in history, but it does not necessarily qualify him to be a school teacher. For that most demanding of all professions, something more is needed.

Respect.

A TEACHING CREDENTIAL IS NOT A LICENSE TO CORRUPT
There are times when sympathy becomes collusion, and when a confidant becomes an accessory ...

If there is one thing practically guaranteed to raise my hackles instantaneously to a 45-degree angle, it is a teacher who deliberately panders to the worst in his students, instead of trying his hardest to bring out the best in them. Fortunately few in number, these prostitutes of my profession deserve to be drummed conspicuously out of education to a Rogue's March of public scorn and private revulsion.

Every so often, one of our more mixed-up instructors will fall by the wayside, betraying his calling in the process. The big black headlines which invariably chronicle the sorry event bear mute testimony to the rarity of the occurrence. Just the same, when it happens, it shouldn't. And it shocks.

A long-haired hippie in my home town of Sacramento recently got picked up by the hard-working constabulary for selling dope to his college classmates. This is par for the course these days, sadly enough, when so many of these grimy misfits are trying convulsively to destroy themselves and everyone around them.

What is emphatically not par for any course and what raised both my ire and my eyebrows simultaneously was the sentimental support given this dope peddler by certain members of his college faculty.

One lady English teacher, apparently still under the narcotic spell of DeQuincey and Coleridge, wrote this sort of unmitigated guff to the trial judge:

"Whatever Mike did, I am sure he did out of love, out of a belief that here was a way to guide people to a truer way of engaging with each other. The law becomes then not a means of justice but a positive hindrance to justice."

Note the implication here. It's all right to break a law in our democratic society if you break it for the sake of love. Laws are thus presumably made for everybody but lovers. And the old lament of the disappointed Frankie just after she has filled Johnny full of lead, "I did it because I loved him," takes on a brand new and highly practical connotation.

When and if I decide to rob a bank, therefore, I have determined to do it with nothing but big, warm, wonderful love in my heart. I may even bestow a gentle kiss upon the flustered brow of the trussed-up bank guard as I step over him with the loot. This should guarantee me a whole flock of character references from my local college faculty. And who knows? Maybe even a demonstration or two down in front of the jail when the cops finally round me up.

Another mortarboarded mumblehead at the same institution lamented to the sorely tried court in regard to this convicted criminal: "His was a search for deeper emotional-spiritual values. He is as much a victim as victimizer."

Next week, same time, same place, "East Lynne."

Sure, he's a victim. So is every scurvy dabbler in drugs who deliberately spreads his own filthy poison to others for the sake of a fast buck. Speaking for myself, I'd a lot rather associate with good old Typhoid Mary. At least she spread only the seeds of physical sickness. She never attempted to destroy the soul.

Come to think of it, I've never read any anguished letters from medical school faculties trying to get poor Mary out of quarantine because she distributed her germs affectionately and with the very best of intentions.

Can it be that our doctors are less sympathetic than our professors? Or just less stupid?

All of us make the laws which govern us. A teacher exists to show his youthful charges how to make desirable changes in those laws in an orderly way.

But a teacher who condones the breaking of democratically enacted laws by those entrusted to his care for any reason on God's earth is not a teacher. Not in my book, anyhow.

He's a Pied Piper of destruction.

TEACHERS   **227**

THE MYTHS OF EDUCATION
Yet there are times when we should stand up on
our hind legs and brag about being teachers . . .

Every profession has suffered at the hands of its caricatur-
ists. My own vocation of teaching has perhaps smarted
more than others.

A century ago, the stereotypes were savage. The male of
my species was universally portrayed as a runty, bald,
slovenly dressed professor who went around with his head
in the clouds and his shoe laces untied, and who was so
absent-minded he regularly scratched his waffles and poured
maple syrup down his back. His female counterpart was
a vinegary, bony, Lydia Pinkham type, with high-button
shoes and a face which would not only have stopped an
eight-day clock but also fused the hands together at high
noon.

With the passage of time, the stereotypes have mellowed
somewhat, but they are still there. Today's masculine instructor is depicted as bespectacled and diffident, sporting
a Herbert Hoover collar and a Phi Beta Kappa key to rein-
force his essential egg-headedness. And the new edition of
the schoolmarm sets forth an earnest, rather gullible image
of a sensibly dressed lady with a 1945 hair-do and ideas to
match.

These cartoon characters are about as true to life as any
others. What I'm concerned with are some of the "idea
stereotypes" which seem to have obtained such a death grip
contemplate the nature of public education. For instance:
upon the American mind when it turns infrequently to

1—*"Teaching is the most radical of the professions."*

This is a real laugh. Aside from the obvious fact that teachers live their lives in a veritable goldfish bowl where a real radical stands out like Cassius Clay in a Quietist monastery and incidentally lasts just about as long, I can personally attest that there is nothing we instructors hate so much as change. Any school principal who has tried to talk a third grade teacher into teaching the fourth grade for a while knows exactly what I mean. He is promptly deluged with complaints about having to develop new lesson plans, collect new material for the bulletin boards and even compose new test questions.

No, teachers are the last to fit the definition of a radical, who is one who desires change at any cost and right now. As I know from experience, educators are all too apt to resist change of any kind, and they resist it not only instinctively but positively viscerally. They are true conservatives, whether they know it or not, and I can't help it if you've run up against a few cap-and-gowned parlor pinks in your time.

2—*"Teachers keep bankers' hours and work only nine months out of the year."*

If you are talking only about time actually spent in the classroom, this is true. If you're talking about time spent correcting papers at home, preparing lessons for tomorrow, coaching the school play and trying to keep up with a rapidly changing profession by going to school all summer, you're all wet. The average teacher works a longer day and a longer year than you do, believe it or not.

3—*"High school teachers work harder than elementary teachers."*

Nope. It's a stand-off. The secondary instructor may have to spend more time at school putting out the yearbook, editing the school paper and keeping order at the football games, but he doesn't have to cope with the three-ring circus complete with various reading groups, workbook circles, and "opportunity clusters" all going full blast and simultaneously with which the grammar school teacher works continuously.

Just in case you've wondered who the most important teacher is, it is the first grade instructor. If she does her job, the kid is apt to have it pretty rosy from then on. If she doesn't, look out!

4—*"He who can, does. He who cannot, teaches."*

When George Bernard Shaw wrote this, he was as jaundiced and smart-alecky and just plain mistaken as he was when he said, "Life is a disease, and the only difference between one man and another is the stage of the disease at which he lives."

A teacher is an artist. He practices the most ancient and incomparably the most important of all the arts. Just as all men are not cut out to be painters and sculptors, neither is every man fitted by nature or temperament to provide succeeding generations with the wonderful, glittering tools and techniques needed to pursue the truth and ensure the survival of civilization.

Shaw be hanged. We teachers not only "can"; we must.

HOW ABOUT A CLOSED SEASON ON TEACHERS?
*And there are other times when we have to band
together and fight in sheer self-defense . . .*

Back in the 10th century the church came up with a convenient custom called the Peace of God, which it imposed
upon the merrily murderous men-at-arms, barons and petty
kings of that day and which for a time it actually made
stick.

Under its terms, noncombatants were declared permanently out of season. Peasants on their way to the communal radish plot, shaven-headed priests on their way to
confession, ladies on their way to wherever it was that
ladies went in those days, were exempted from the general
slaughter and were allowed to holler "King's X!" whenever
some knightly nut started after them with lowered lance
and visor.

Sheer survival for certain essential population segments
was the goal, and I'd like here and now to extend the
principle to my own particular population segment in this,
the seventh decade of the 20th century.

How about a closed season on teachers? For a while,
anyhow. Long enough at least for us to recover our morale
and regroup our forces a little.

It's a rare edition of your daily paper which doesn't
contain somewhere between the front page and the want
ads a story about some unsuspecting instructor getting
clobbered by a petulant pupil, a peevish parent or just a
casual member of the lay public looking for some patsy on
whom to vent his frustrations. In several of our Eastern

cities, teacher has to be escorted home from work by burly members of the gendarmerie. In other itchy locales, the hapless pedagogue who agrees to teach Negroes gets way-laid by whites, and if he doesn't agree to teach Negroes he gets chased out of town by blacks.

In my home state, several teachers were flushed out of their once-quiet classrooms by a roaring mob and sent to the hospital with assorted lacerations, contusions and fractures. The brawling rioters were protesting alleged de facto segregation, they said, and were quite taken aback when the local teachers' association complained about the excessively physical nature of the protest. After all, the Great Society was conceived in demonstrations and spawned in violence, wasn't it?

How else ya gonna git Whitey to listen? Or Blacky? Huh?

The fact that the invaded instructors had about as much to say in regard to their school board's racial policies as I have about the Vietnam war strategy didn't deter the slobbish assailants one whit. Neither did the hard-earned and generally justified reputation of my profession for treating all children with exact fairness and even with rueful affection, equally distributed.

No. The school is there, open and defenseless. It is manned by scholars who are usually pretty gentle people, devoted to reason and persuasion, not to fisticuffs. So let's go in and roust 'em around a little. After all, we pay 'em, don't we? Why should they squawk?

So goes the current refrain.

Oh, we've always been a violent nation. And as anyone who has read "The Hoosier Schoolmaster" knows, teachers have from time to time been forced to lick the biggest kid in the class in order to establish the right to teach him Latin conjugations or geometrical axioms.

But the Sick Sixties Syndrome is something brand new. Never before in our history have mobs attacked the schools and those who keep education's flag flying in the teeth of increasingly hostile gales. Never before has it been seriously proposed that karate be made a part of teacher training, as has been proposed to me in California.

Well, we school people have just about had it. In my state we introduced legislation which makes it so expensive and so confining and so downright disastrous to make a punching bag out of a teacher that even the most sullen and stupid slob will think twice before he starts beating on Miss Brooks with a tire iron.

The sad part is that it's necessary. Sadder still is the sick society it mirrors.

When do we start equipping priests with pistols? Or the Salvation Army with shotguns?

A FEW THINGS EDUCATION BADLY NEEDS
But once in a while we should take a long look at ourselves, and comb the kooks out of our hair . . .

Education, which is at least the second-oldest profession, needs a fairy godmother these days worse than Cinderella did the night of the ball. If we educators do have one—and in these Great Society times everybody has at least one—I wish the old girl would materialize from her never-never land of chalk, pencils and old N.E.A. bulletins long enough to grant us the customary three wishes.

There are lots of things schoolmen need, of course, like more money, stronger nerves and a less equivocal public image. But if I really had my druthers, here are the three I'd pick:

1—*A good, healthy sense of humor with special emphasis on willingness to laugh hilariously at ourselves once in a while.*

Sadly enough, education has of late become the most humorless of all the professions. Compared to us, lawyers are convulsive cards, doctors are compulsive kidders and even the longest-faced fundamentalist preacher is a regular Red Skelton.

This is a strange turn of events, historically speaking. Ever since frontier days the schoolmaster and the school-marm have served to provide much that is friendly and familiar in American humor. And nearly all the teachers I've known have had a pretty healthy sense of the ridiculous, if only because our highly exacting and more than somewhat nerve-racking calling too often gives its practitioners only the all-out choice between a gust of laughter or a torrent of tears.

I really blame our umpteen teachers' unions, organizations and associations for education's currently dead-pan public image. Too many of their public relations people act and look as though they had been weaned on a pickle.

Come on, fellows. Let's laugh it up a little.

2—*Ability to see ourselves and our problems in proper perspective.*

The world isn't really coming to an end, you know.

True, we teachers have to get an entire generation ready for the Age of the Computer and for manned flights to Mars. But to travel backward down the years for just a moment, our predecessors had to prepare their bright-eyed and often hell-raising charges for such things as intercontinental wars, the saving of the Union, westward expansion and the original separation from Great Britain, for that matter.

They succeeded pretty well and, oddly enough, without any national "master plan" for benevolently directed educational policy, either.

Suppose we've lost the knack?

3—*A badly needed recommitment to fundamental democratic procedures.*

I'm sick of booing, hissing, facially contorted, fist-swinging punks in caps and gowns serving as examples to our children.

Educators should be the strongest supporters of due process and parliamentary procedure in the land. Our whole profession depends upon society's staying on track and not careening all over the landscape in a querulous quest for civil disobedience, LSD, draft card burning, black power and what have you.

Instead, some of our nuttier members seem dedicated to chaos. In February of 1967, I witnessed the miserably bad taste displayed by some members of the American Federation of Teachers who led a gaggle of their loudmouthed pupils in an organized out-shouting of California's brand-new governor on his own doorstep. If the best we educators can do for the next generation is to teach them to substitute lung power for brain power, maybe we should quit and let the campus yell leaders take over in our place.

I'm reminded, in fact, that the Fascists have always been great booers, hooters and spitters. They like to drown out all opposing arguments with a minimum of logic and a maximum of red-faced blat, punctuated with the satisfying, flesh-smacking blows of rubber truncheons judiciously applied.

I think the rest of us teachers had better step up our quiet and effective fight against this sorry syndrome and cast an increasingly jaundiced eye on these loose nuts among us who seem recently to have picked up the academic ball and run away with it at our expense.

Come to think of it, Joe Goebbels was a schoolteacher. Remember?

Apparently he has left some spiritual descendants.

GROUP XIII

Miscellaneous

None of these fitted in anywhere.

They just made a place for themselves.

IT'S NOT THE TURMOIL THESE DAYS: IT'S THE ENNUI
Some things that bug me . . .

I think it was Cardinal Newman who partially defined the truly educated man as one who is never bored. If so, I'm afraid the cardinal would drum me out of the ranks of the literati because a lot of things these days bore the heck out of me. For instance:

Overnight conscientious objectors

I can generate a certain sympathy for the Quaker who has been taught since birth never to take human life and who remains true to his religious beliefs, despite the obvious fact that if all Americans shared his philosophy our nation over the years would have writhed under the respective heels of George III, Santa Anna, Kaiser Wilhelm, Adolf Hitler and Joe Stalin.

But I can produce nothing except a cavernous yawn for the hippie who spends his life scoffing blasphemously at God, morality and the human soul, only to develop instant scruples when he is about to get drafted. His piteous plea that a conscience which he has never previously acknowledged is now pricking him so sorely that he should be excused from military service leaves me icy-cold.

Swinging priests

There seems to be a mad rush of late to tuck religion into the same bed with Hugh Hefner, Joan Baez and Bertrand Russell. Hotly pursuing this far-out goal of wholesale spiritual miscegenation, certain men of the cloth are currently busy renouncing everything their faith has ever stood for and in the process are discarding all canons of decency and ordinary good taste.

Anything goes for these swingers in reversed collars, it seems. In Los Angeles they want collective bargaining, like so many longshoremen. In San Francisco they put on cute little dancing parties for practicing homosexuals. In New York they discuss what or whom to substitute for God now that they have decided He is dead. In England they turn the church over to a rock-'n'-roll combo while the congregation dances the Watusi in front of the altar.

Usually I'm not one to solicit divine thunderbolts as an antidote to boredom, but in the case of these paltry prelates I'll be happy to make an exception.

Demonstrating for the sake of demonstrating

I wonder how many of my fellow countrymen are as sick as I am of the traffic tie-ups, the highway blocking, the police-baiting, the vapid placards and the general aura of unwashed disinhibition exuding from these bearded characters who have apparently adopted demonstrating as a lifelong career.

Before the national legislation and the Supreme Court decisions of recent years, demonstrations may have had some logical purpose. But the laws are now on the books. What's needed today is a general improvement in the way people think and feel about each other.

I happen to believe that education can work this improvement. I have Everest-size doubts that demonstrations can. And besides, they're getting to be so confoundedly dull.

"Adult" entertainment

This is a fancy name for pretentious smut. The producers of this smirking, sniggering pornography like to pontificate solemnly that they are dealing bravely with the issues of today and with themes fresh from the mint of modernity.

Somehow, apparently, the seventh decade of the 20th century is unlike any of the countless others which have preceded it in history and, therefore, must be portrayed on stage and screen with relentlessly sweaty realism, using the vocabulary of a Skid Row bum.

Horsefeathers.

What these muck merchants really mean is that our rapidly relaxing moral fiber is affording them a not-to-be-missed opportunity to make a fast and filthy buck.

I don't mind a self-confessed and cheerful rogue. He usually keeps me awake, at least.

I do mind a slimy and sententious hypocrite. He never does.

TO SKIP OR NOT TO SKIP
If I may wax personal for a moment or two . . .

Once upon a time there was a little boy called Johnny Know-It-All. His teacher didn't know what to do with him.

He was a fourth grader, but he was reading Dickens while his classmates were still putting syllables together.

He knew all about the Peloponnesian War and could recite the capital of every country in the world while the other kids were locating the continents on the Mercator projection. Result: He was bored stiff.

Conscientious Miss Appleby was concerned. Not only was her owl-eyed young charge beginning to give her the creeps, but also he was showing signs of the classic Sid Sawyer Syndrome: pride, prissiness and poisonous politeness.

Dialogue with school principal:

Miss A.: The boy's not being challenged.

Principal: Put him where he will be.

Miss A.: You mean . . . ?

Principal: (firmly but kindly): Skip him to a higher grade.

Which is about as logical as would be this kind of a conversation:

Miss A.: The boy's only 8, but he's strong as an ox. He can lift any two of his classmates right off the floor.

Principal: So put him where he can't do this to his classmates. Sign him up with the Chicago Bears.

There were a few other things about Johnny that cried for consideration and didn't get it, you see.

One was that he didn't really know it all. His arithmetic was mediocre. Ditto science.

Another was that he was already a year younger than his classmates and showed it in a lot of ways. Seems he had "skipped" kindergarten a few years back because he could already read when he started school.

Johnny's so-called giftedness really boiled down to the fact that he was a good reader.

It's not enough. Believe me.

Oh, he got skipped again, of course. And from then on he was two years younger than anybody and two years smaller and many, many more than two years sadder.

In junior high his weakness in arithmetic caught up with him, and he turned into a mathematical cripple. He still is. He learned to bluff it out. He still does.

High school boxed him in neatly. He was a freak, an object of simultaneous envy and derision at an age where such treatment is exquisite agony.

College just about finished the job. He was admitted to the university at the ripe old age of 15. Voices sounded through his undergraduate days and echo still through the mist of all the years between the Then and Now.

Football? "Want the kid to get killed?"

Dates? "He's such a cute little fellow, but go out with him? Really, my dear!"

Fraternities? "We're not rushing babies. Yet."

Campus politics? "Come off it. We're not after the junior high vote."

Result? All the doors were slammed and locked. Except the ones marked Grind and Bookworm. So that's what he became. The carefree college days which most of us look back on through the indescribable glow which hedges around the name of Alma Mater were driven, wincing, hellish days for Johnny.

My point, I think, is made. The erstwhile prodigy in the fullness of time went from bad to worse, like a modern version of "The Drunkard," and in the end became a part-time newspaper columnist, which as everyone knows is a destiny far worse than death.

Sadly enough, he could have been saved if his teacher had been willing and able to enrich his learning pattern instead of cold-bloodedly interrupting it and lifting him out of it. He needed special help, not alienation. Understanding, not separation.

Be warned, ye pedagogues and parents, by this boy's fearful fate. And when someone mentions "skipping" (or, more euphemistically "accelerating") to you, punch him right smack on the nose.

I know. You see, I was that boy. Johnny Know-It-All, who really didn't. And for quite a spell I was miserable beyond the bourn of all imaginings.

IT'S TIME FOR THE EDUCATIONAL WEED-KILLER AGAIN
How to make education totalitarian . . .

Voltaire had some wise words about the importance of cultivating one's garden, and in my line of work it's especially vital. Every so often it's a good idea to turf out some of the particularly obnoxious weeds which masquerade as sweet-smelling violets in the garden of education.

Here are a few of the tares and thistles, currently manured with the compost of collectivism, cross-pollinated by the assiduous spreaders of the Gospel According to St. John Dewey, and flowering all over the place in the pious platitudes and corny clichés so dear to some members of my profession.

All of them, incidentally, are as phony as a Peking peace feeler. Recognize them?

1—"Education has become too important to be left any longer to the states and to the local school districts. The energizing influence and infinitely richer resources of the federal government must be brought increasingly into the educational picture."

This is a jabberwocky way of saying "Big Brother wants Junior."

As you hear increasingly during the months and years ahead about "federal goals for education," "national educational compacts," "establishment of nationwide educational standards" and other clackings of the same ilk, just bear in mind the saying above. In the long run, they all boil down to this:

Big Brother wants Junior. And the younger the better.

Local grass-roots education needs to be energized, modernized and personalized, true enough. It does *not* need to be subsidized, nepotized and zombieized, at least not by Uncle Sam in his favorite Great Society role as Mr. Fix-It.

2—"A racially integrated school is a better school than a segregated school."

As Gershwin once said about something else, "It ain't necessarily so." All other things being equal, yes. Things like good teachers, interesting books, challenging curriculum and decent facilities, for example. If both schools are getting the same break insofar as these prime essentials are concerned, then certainly the integrated one is better.

But if School No. 1 has any or all of these things, and if School No. 2 doesn't, then all bets are off. You can integrate No. 2 right down to the last perfectly balanced computer decimal place and it will still be an educational lemon as compared to No. 1.

3—"The school exists to make the child an adjusted, accepted member of his peer group."

Nope. As I've said somewhere before, the school exists to make him learned. Period.

4—"The solution to present-day school problems lies in constructing huge, elaborately planned educational parks or plazas in centralized locations and bussing the children to them from miles away."

Certainly. That is, if you want your kids to go to school in a far-off educational factory where they will be schooled scientifically by trained and kindly experts without any ignorant, bumbling interference from little old you.

But if you are carpingly small-minded enough to want Susie to get her schooling where you can have some kind of a say in what that schooling is going to be—if you hanker to visit the teacher once in a while, or even if you just want to be able to get hold of Susie fast in case of an emergency—then you'd better hang onto your humdrum little neighborhood school, despite the fact that it's rapidly getting to be a naughty word in some sociological circles.

And if one of our educational bureaucrats, resplendently sent among us from his Washington superiors to convert the heathen out in the hinterland, tells you with that air of insufferable condescension which is the badge and hallmark of his tribe that the neighborhood school is relatively inefficient compared to his precious educational "plaza," inform him that a democracy is relatively inefficient, too, compared to any well-run ant hill, beehive or Hitlerian dictatorship.

Then look him straight in the eye and ask, "So what?"

THE HIPPIES AND THE HERMITS: HISTORICAL PARALLEL
*The Flower Children. Parasites who make fun
of their host . . .*

The Hippie Phenomenon.

We are currently appraising it gingerly, and with all
the wide-eyed wonder of astronauts touching down upon
the terra incognita of an uncharted planet.

How odd of us. Because the Bathless Groggins Syndrome
isn't new, you know. As a matter of fact, it's at least 1500
years old.

Just to demonstrate once again that there's nothing really
new under the sun, let's hop aboard the time machine of
history and set the dials for 5th century North Africa.
After the sand settles from our touchdown, we are going
to feel right at home, at least with respect to one part of our
environment.

For we shall find ourselves viewing with a distinct shock
of recognition a small but highly publicized segment of the
local population which has withdrawn unto itself in the
wake of Rome's crumbling culture and which has set up
little sun-drenched desert sanctuaries for some very weird
birds indeed.

The men wear uncut beards and sandals, the women long,
straggly hair and a bemused expression. Both sexes speak
an "in" jargon all their own. Both profess superabundant
love for everybody and everything in sight, including the
taciturn Nilotic crocodiles. And, unlike the crocodiles, both
bathe so seldom that the wary traveler can smell one of
their little settlements long before he can see it.

Sound vaguely familiar?

They are the flotsam and jetsam of a vast imperial ship-wreck. Despairing of influencing their more humdrum and prosaic fellow citizens, they have seceded from them. Rather than bear the banner of civilization into combat against the encroaching hordes of barbarians, they have deliberately elected to go the barbarians one better by wallowing so wholeheartedly in the slough of barbarism that no self-respecting Goth or Vandal would go within sniffing distance of them.

Most of these "turned on" ones spend long, vapid life-times exploiting some personal peculiarity, often with de-cided overtones of masochism. Thus I read with a sense of déja-vu about a certain Haight-Ashbury hippie who skew-ered a hole in his chest skin without benefit of anesthesia so he could install an earring. He would have felt right at home a millenium and a half ago with old Simeon Stylites who starved himself periodically for 40 years while existing precariously atop a narrow-based, 50-foot pillar. Or with one of Simeon's creepier Egyptian colleagues who kept his fist clenched until his fingernails had grown right through the back of his hand.

As we peer through our time machine's portholes we can't help but be struck with a remarkable and even eerie resemblance between the hermits and the hippies.

Both practice mysticism and chant gnomic incantations amid surroundings unsanitary enough to make a pig blush.

Both preach peace at any price, avoid military service like the plague and rely blissfully on their less sophisticated and more public-spirited countrymen to defend them from a hard-boiled, no-nonsense enemy from overseas.

And both contain within their bedraggled ranks large numbers of arrant exhibitionists who will do anything from wrestling publicly with highly subjective fiends fresh from a purely hypothetical pit then, to cultivating Fu Manchu mustachios for the titillation of Sunday San Francisco tourists now.

The hermits of the Dark Ages sprang from a sick society and were living symptoms of it. I leave it to you, gentle reader, to determine what our 20th century hippies are symptoms of.

One ironic footnote to history, for what it may be worth.

Shortly after our Wellsian tour back through time, the hermit colonies were wiped out, root and branch, by the militant, fanatical and highly organized Muslims, led by the heirs of a certain leader named Muhammed. These were certainly a cleaner people, if not perhaps quite so interested in love, nonviolence and showing off.

Come to think of it, I've come across something like them fairly recently, too.

Isn't history fascinating? Sometimes a little scary, though. Especially when it decides to repeat itself.

GULLIVER'S SIZE DIDN'T MAKE HIM SMARTER
*Every day in at least one way we're getting
bigger and bigger . . .*

There is very little correlation between size and intelligence. Unfortunately. Because we the people are getting bigger every generation. Physically.

One of our eastern universities has sent a graduating class into each of three great wars, and vital statistics are available. The class of 1917 was almost two inches taller and 20 pounds heavier than its blue-clad predecessor of 1861. And the GI graduates of 1942 averaged another inch higher and 10 pounds weightier than their dads.

I had this phenomenon brought home sharply to me the other day when I visited the armor collection in New York's Metropolitan Museum. Out of the hundreds of metal suits dating back to the 14th century, I could have squeezed into exactly three. And I'm not really built like Charles Atlas.

The gauntlets and sollerets were made for hands and feet not found upon this earth today, save possibly among the diminutive inhabitants of Southeast Asia. But the big shocker came when I viewed the very few damask and brocaded gowns which have come down to us, almost miraculously preserved, from the days of Elizabeth and Mary, Queen of Scots. The fair damsels of chivalric legend were little bigger than dolls, apparently.

Yet the two-handed swords and battle-axes on display are demonstrably massive, not to be twirled lightly about one's head even by a modern Olympic athlete. Our forebears must have been muscled like so many pint-sized Percherons.

When you think about this a little, it figures. Even in our own brief life span we've seen whatever it is that's happening to us. I don't think my old high school had more than one 200-pounder on its whole football team. Today, the coach gets out the crying towel if his defensive line doesn't average at least 205. And our professional guards and tackles would simply confirm our ancestors in their unshakeable belief in ogres and giants if they were vouchsafed one horrified look at Coach Halas' "Monsters of the Midway."

Track and field marks in our own time so far surpass the best efforts of 50 years ago as to make our grandfathers look ludicrous. Part of this is no doubt due to better coaching, improved training methods and more scientific conditioning, but not all of it, by any means. The human body is bigger, stronger and faster than it used to be.

Why?

The popular explanation is that we're giving kids more milk, nicely pasteurized and irradiated, than we used to. Vitamins, minerals and proteins share the credit with sunlight, fresh air and better doctors. And I suppose that a century from now our descendants will be inclined to attribute the whole thing to Medicare and the Great Society.

I don't believe a word of it.

Our pioneer forefathers got one heck of a lot more sunlight and fresh air—yes, and fresh food—than we get today. Their relatively high death rate stemmed largely from the fact that they knew nothing of the germ theory of disease and had a regrettable habit of building their privies entirely too close to their wells. Half their babies died before they reached the age of five, mostly because of ignorance.

Similarly, we lose an appalling percentage of our population today to accidents, cancer and heart disease, often at an embarrassingly early age. We foul up our atmosphere with smog, our rivers and lakes with sewage and our soil with strontium fallout. Again, mostly because of ignorance.

Neither set of mortality statistics impresses me as being a reasonable cause either of our ancestors' small size or our own comparative giantism. If you ask me, we've got a mutational trend running, similar in some ways to the trend which ran about the year 10,000 B.C., when *genus homo*, who had been happily and hairily living in caves for hundreds of thousands of years with little visible change, suddenly emerged into the sunlight and started building pyramids and carving Abu Simbel.

It would be nice if Providence would arrange a corresponding jump in our mental and artistic potential to go along with our added pounds and inches, wouldn't it?

I suppose this is too much to expect, though.

By the way, have you noticed how big women's feet are getting?

A GOOD WORD FOR CAPITAL PUNISHMENT
*I'm pretty unregenerate about this. Instead of doing
away with the gas chamber, I think we ought
to enlarge it . . .*

Jefferson used to say that government should do only those things for the individual which the individual by the very nature of things couldn't do for himself. I would like to suggest presumptuously the addition of the subordinate clause: "and which the individual *shouldn't* do for himself."

For instance, the punishment of crime. You heard me. I said "punishment."

Not rehabilitation, salvaging or even reclamation. Punishment.

When Uk the Neolithic hunter came home after a hard day's pursuit of the elusive mammoth to find that his glowering neighbor Guk had taken over his cave and for good measure had bashed his wife's skull in with a stone ax, he didn't call the cops or swear out a warrant. He went after Guk himself and laid the wood to him personally, thus permanently insuring Guk's future nonparticipation in crime.

Starting about 4000 B.C., society took over the function of avengement from us individual and usually undermuscled Uks, and made it unnecessary for us to pay back our ghastliest wrongs in kind. The blood feud went out of style. So did family ambushes, trial by combat and, eventually, the duel.

Until quite recently, in fact, this was one of the surefire ways of telling a civilized man from a savage. But today, society seems about to go out of this line of work. More and more states are currently abdicating their immemorial chore of getting Guk off our backs. And our courts of late have become one heck of a lot more concerned with poor, frustrated, bloodthirsty Guk than they are with the rest of us law-abiding and increasingly terrorized unfortunates who look to the law to keep Guk from slicing our throats while we sleep.

Never mind if some surly slob blasts his neighbor with a shotgun. He's probably just discharging some pent-up aggression dating back to his childhood days when someone locked him in a dark closet overlong. He's not responsible.

And don't be beastly to some brute who stomps a polio victim to death in a dark alley for kicks. It's not his fault. He's sick.

Maybe so. But in my state as well as a good many others, a lot of us are scared stiff to be caught out after dark in the heart of our greatest cities. This goes double for our women. And I don't know about you, but I'm not—I repeat, *not*—paying taxes for this.

Oh, I'm as sympathetic as the next man with the poor misunderstood murderer. But I'm a lot more sympathetic with his rapidly growing number of victims, especially when statistics show I'm increasingly apt to become one of them.

I suggest we get our states back into the business of lowering the boom on Guk. Permanently. Nothing, incidentally, accomplishes this task half so well as capital punishment, promptly and vigorously applied.

Oh, I know. The psychologists all say that it doesn't deter, that it's barbarous and that punishment should be shelved in favor of rehabilitation.

Capital punishment may not deter potential criminals, but there's one thing for sure: it certainly deters the criminal who receives it. He'll never swing any more axes.

Capital punishment may be barbarous. Not nearly so barbarous as murder.

Capital punishment makes rehabilitation impossible. True. But ever since time began, there has been a thing called retribution, which followed evil doing as day follows night, and rightly so. If organized society doesn't provide it, the individual will, just so long as the human race remains human.

We are justly proud of eliminating lynching in America. Let us not set the stage for its hideous return by taking the power of life and death away from the state, and the fear which is the beginning of wisdom out of the murky minds of murderers.

"Whosoever sheddeth man's blood, by man shall his blood be shed."

Shocking sentiment, eh Guk? Ferocious, too.

Funny thing though. It'll never bother you one bit if you use that ax on nothing but kindling wood.

EDUCATION'S UNEXPECTED ENEMY: TELEVISION
Ode to the Boob Tube . . .

Each time a bunch of educators gets together at a convention, a lot of pious claptrap is voiced about the marvelous manner in which television is seconding and supporting the work of the schools. Every hoary cliché in the book is dragged out and resuscitated, from one picture being worth a thousand you-know-whats to the family where TV is viewed together staying glued together.

The industry sends a couple of its slickest public relations men over to con the school people out of a few more touching testimonials, and a general air of reciprocal self-satisfaction hangs smugly over all.

Bunk.

Television could be the greatest boon to education since the discovery of chalk, but it isn't. For every edifying exception like "Michelangelo" or "The Louvre," there is a whole torrent of audiovisual rubbish which not only submerges real education in a spate of glittering garbage, but also acts corrosively on the instructional process itself.

For instance:

Television sneaks up on real history and blackjacks it almost every night. We've been regaled with a weekly series on Daniel Boone showing that homespun hero hobnobbing with all kinds of people the real Boone never heard of, including a British general.

Jesse James, who was a bad one if there ever was one, is portrayed as a cross between Galahad and St. Francis of Assisi. Heaven help the poor history teacher faced with this kind of competition!

For a while I thought the idiot box might actually revive public interest in the grand old subject of Greek and Roman mythology. Well, it did, in a way. Now we have a generation of youngsters growing up believing that Hercules and Ulysses were contemporaries and went around slaying hydras together, thanks to the almost incredibly bad Italian movies which TV shows so proudly every Saturday afternoon.

Literature is prostituted coldly and deliberately right in our living rooms to the point where its ancient muse resembles nothing so much as a somewhat bedraggled call girl. Anyone who ever read Owen Wister's "The Virginian," for example, remembers Trampas as the contumelious villain whose unprintable cuss-word evoked the Virginian's immortal response: "When you call me that, smile!" On television, Trampas is a hero.

But it is the English language which so far has been television's most conspicuous and badly mauled victim. It is pretty tough to have to teach the proper use of the subjective pronoun in the classroom to kids who spend the rest of their waking hours having "Us smokers would rather fight than switch" dinned into their ears.

And the valuable distinction between those two useful little words "like" and "as" has been brutally murdered by the tireless efforts of one tobacco manufacturer to persuade us that his product "tastes good like a cigarette should."

I'm no pedant, but it does seem to me that the moguls who mastermind this billion-dollar industry can do better than this. In fact, it's hard to imagine how anyone could do worse.

I guess the thing which really bugs me, as the kids say, is the blithe arrogance of an attitude which takes for granted the highly dubious assumption that it can improve on history, rewrite literature, ignore grammar and create a new mythology, when in reality these Madison Ave. hucksters are in the same general literary league as Cassius Clay.

The whole thing reminds me of a Hollywood movie made back in the Thirties. It was "Romeo and Juliet," and the credit blurb read "By William Shakespeare, with additional dialogue by Joe Glotz."

THE EMBATTLED PTA
*And a kind word about an overly
maligned institution . . .*

We have always been a nation prone to stereotypes and caricatures. Professors are invariably absent-minded. Old maids are perpetually hoping for burglars under their beds.

Men with strong backs universally suffer from weak minds. And PTA meetings are uniformly dull.

When you stop to think, it's strange that an organization so all-inclusive as the PTA and so concerned with such an interesting subject as education should have been tagged so long with the label of boredom. Husbands down through the years have reputedly tried every trick in the book, from acute indigestion to too many martinis, to avoid the monthly gatherings at Witherspoon Elementary School. The financial reports would put Argus himself to sleep, and the cookie sales follow one another with the maddening monotony of Southeast Asian governments. So runs the myth.

Well, I have news for you. Whether it was ever thus, it's not any more. For the past two or three years a typical PTA meeting has been about as tedious as the landing on Omaha Beach.

It all started, I suppose, with Admiral Rickover's amphibious attack, complete with rockets and napalm, upon the surprised and somewhat sluggish association. Demonstrating a brand of sheer, chome-steel nerve, which I presume has been standard equipment for naval heroes ever since the days of John Paul Jones, the good admiral referred daringly to the ladies of the PTA as "infernal nuisances," and suggested strongly that they stay home in the future and busy themselves with cooking dinners for their husbands.

At about this same time the association came under a barrage laid down by enraged conservatives who claimed that the state and national hierarchies were meddling increasingly in politics. The PTA, it seems, was sponsoring federal aid to education bills, pushing civil rights legislation and even taking positions on statewide initiative measures which had little or nothing to do with education.

More recently, the embattled national president of the parents and teachers launched an attack of her own, this time on the John Birch Society, which she claims is trying to infiltrate PTA and take it over, lock, stock and barrel.

Somehow I can't seem to get very excited about this whole thing. I've probably sat in on as many PTA meetings in my time as any man living, and if there is one thing I'm certain of, it is that they are all different. Some local chapters are active, alert and full of ideas. Others are as dull as the mythical stereotype makes them out to be. It all depends on how much the community is interested in helping its kids and how willing Mom and Pop are to tear themselves away from television once a month in order to try and create a better school climate from which Junior can benefit.

If your PTA is boring, it's because you haven't insisted on some bang-up controversial programs.

If PTA is meddling in politics when it shouldn't, it's because you have permitted it to and, in some cases, encouraged it to.

If the Birchers are trying to take over your school chapter, possibly it's because they are the only individuals in your community who are interested enough in education to care one hoot who runs the show.

Every school needs parents and teachers working together for the good of the children. To paraphrase Voltaire—if PTA did not exist, it would be necessary to invent it. The proof is that wherever it has been done away with it has sooner or later been replaced by an almost identical organization boasting a somewhat different combination of initials.

There's nothing wrong with PTA except you and me. And, incidentally, that is true of the whole community.

THE DROPOUT PUZZLE

I'm not sure what to do about the dropout problem. But I'm pretty sure what NOT to do about it . . .

Every generation of man develops its own brand of escapism. The old Greeks created the *deus ex machina* by means of which Sophocles and Euripides solved hopeless dramatic contretemps by summoning the "god from the machine," who would descend from Olympus at the end of the last act and tidy everything up.

The ancient Hebrews relied upon convenient and sometimes indiscriminate miracles on the part of a highly accessible Jehovah. Our medieval forebears invented fairy god-mothers and magic wands to extricate them from insoluble difficulties. The Victorians had a charming, if child-like, faith that science would sooner or later provide the answer to every human problem, from politics to predestination.

Our current magic wand is legislation, with several hundred hard-boiled congressmen and state legislators cast in the unlikely role of fairy godmother.

Is there a nasty, baffling puzzle lurking anywhere on the horizon? Pass a law—and get rid of it.

Does an issue which has stumped our best brains for generations still stalk the land, wailing aloud for a solution? Relax. A good stiff statute will settle its hash.

Kind of makes you wonder why our ancestors were so stupid as not to have come up with this easy, painless cure-all a long time ago, doesn't it?

Actually, of course, they did. Back in 1918 they reared back and passed the 18th Amendment, which solved permanently and at one stroke the moral and educational enigma of strong drink. And everyone knows how successful that solution has been over the years. Inexplicably, however, they failed to follow through after this brilliant breakthrough.

Currently, it's the dropout problem for which statutory cure is being sought. In several states the proposal has been made recently that we eliminate early high school terminations by simply requiring all youngsters to remain in school until their 18th birthdays. By law. Just like that. Simple, isn't it?

Despite the fact that laws always solve everything, however, certain nagging questions come to mind.

Will this solution attack the cause? Will it find the reason why kids don't want to stay in school and do something about it? What about the 6-foot, 200-pound 17-year-old who shows up in Miss Frisby's literature class under the new law, puts his motorcycle boots up on his desk, twirls his switchblade and growls: "All right, you old bat. I'm here. Let's see you teach me something"?

What's the law going to do with him? Paddle him? It would take five grown men just to hold him down. Expel him? That's what he wants. Send him to jail? But that's what the new legislation is designed to prevent.

No, what we have to do is explore the "why" of early dropouts. We need desperately to know the reason school gradually ceases to have any meaning to 25% of our young people. Several states, including my own, are presently far advanced in such vital research. Maybe after we obtain this crucial answer we can manage to do without the magic wands and the fairy godmothers.

Since this time we are dealing with kids in and out of school instead of with adults in and out of saloons, perhaps we can overcome the temptation to pass another 18th Amendment.

Just this once?

Maybe?

THE CASE AGAINST
NATIONAL EDUCATIONAL PLANNING
This one will insure my lasting popularity
in Washington . . .

National goals for education are all the rage these days. We educators are being told on all sides to get together under the federal aegis, coordinate the school curricula of the several states in the interests of increased efficiency and generally to plan ahead for a more uniform end-product issuing from the nation's schools.

Why?

Who the devil wants a uniform end-product? I don't.

I am familiar with the rationalizations currently being batted about like so many bright and bromidic balloons:

the different educational standards prevailing in various corners of the country; the need to produce more highly trained technicians if we are to continue to compete in tomorrow's world; the waste implicit in the spectacle of a great nation mounting its educational steed like Stephen Leacock's famous horseman and riding madly off in all directions.

If it weren't for the fact that I have a well-known aversion to badgering my distinguished colleagues, the so-called "leaders" of American education, I would be sorely tempted to lump these specious products of their collective thinking under the general heading of piffle.

We built out of a primeval wilderness a nation which is at once the wonder and the envy of mankind, and we did it without any national goals for education at all.

We have more and better scientists and technicians than any other country in the world. Our gross national product is superior to anybody else's by umpteen hundred per cent. Our satellites fly just as far and just as fast as anybody else's. All this, oddly enough, without Big Brother in Washington directing or even "coordinating" what goes on in our thousands of local school districts in the 50 states.

Why, then, are we getting all this guff nowadays about how badly the country needs guidance and direction from an all-wise, Olympian national council or agency which in the Alice-in-Wonderland jargon of the day will "overview" the problem and provide an "ongoing, forward-looking format" for the future?

To be brutally frank, we are getting it because Big Brother has decided it's time to move in on education

and take over. I suppose it was unreasonable for us educators to sit by simultaneously watching everything else
in the country devoured by Washington and thinking
that somehow we were going to miraculously escape join-
ing all the other Jonahs in the belly of the federal whale.

Just the same, the complete lack of authority for this
sort of muscling in on local school districts is pointed
up by the thunderous silence of our Constitution in regard to education. The word itself appears nowhere in
that distinguished document, indicating clearly enough
even to the most myopic that education is one of the
"residual" powers which the Founding Fathers intended
to leave strictly to the states.

The fact is that Madison and Company would as soon
have contemplated hellfire and the pit as to have coun-
tenanced a national system of education. They knew what
we should know but apparently don't: that as soon as a
vast federal bureaucracy gets its cold, clammy hands on
local schooling, education ceases to be education and
becomes something quite, quite different.

Unfortunately, a Supreme Court which can conjure
up out of nowhere the power to reapportion state legisla-
tures can doubtless dream up some reason to legalize
federal meddling in local school systems.

We don't need national "goals" for education. All we
need is a commitment by educators themselves that each
child needs to be schooled up to his maximum potential
and that effective instruction in organized, disciplined,
systematic subject matter is the only thing which in the
years ahead will stand between this nation and atomized

destruction. Such a commitment does not require Big Brother and his bureaucracy; all it requires is common sense.

There is nothing wrong with the states cooperating among themselves to further the cause of better education. But we had better be mighty careful how we turn our educational planning over to anybody but ourselves.

Otherwise education is apt to end up like the well-known young lady from Niger who went for a ride on a tiger and returned from the ride with the lady inside and a smile on the face of the tiger.

ON THE GROWING THINNESS OF PUBLIC SKINS
"Sticks and stones . . ."

Have you noticed how thin-skinned our public figures are turning these days?

You may recall that in days of yore when a fellow became either prominent or notorious he took it for granted that he would automatically be setting himself up as a living, perambulating target for the slings and arrows of outrageous criticism. More, he had every reason to anticipate downright abuse from John Q. Public, and he usually got it.

As a result, the public figure either developed an almost impenetrable rhinoceros hide before he wandered into the limelight of popular notice, or he took care to develop one shortly afterward out of sheer self-preservation, if nothing else.

George Washington, for example, commented mildly at one point that the press of his day was wont to describe him in terms usually reserved for a common burglar. This, however, did not prevent the father of his country from serving two full terms as President, and without audibly blubbering with self-pity or bawling with indignation.

Abe Lincoln long treasured a front-page cartoon portraying him as an orangutan, hanging from a tree branch and ecstatically scratching himself. Old Abe used to exhume this charming tribute to his manly beauty and gaze at it reflectively whenever he was tempted to feel overly pleased with himself. But I never heard of his suing anybody or even hiring a lawyer to protect him against what was surely one of the most vicious torrents of abuse ever unleashed against anyone, any time, anywhere.

Performers of that day, too, willy-nilly donned the same protective armor of stoical acceptance. In an age when disapproval of one's Thespian abilities involved not only poor press notices, but also an uninhibited application af old eggs and dead cats from the first three rows of orchestra seats, the theater was no place for the bashful, blushing introvert.

Things have changed, and more than somewhat.

We have been regaled with the piquant spectacle of Joan Baez threatening to sue cartoonist Al Capp for daring to caricature her, Sen. Thomas Dodd protesting because someone was looking into his visible and not-so-visible means of support, Adam Clayton Powell proclaiming that the land of the free and home of the brave had suddenly collapsed because his fellow congressmen had rebuked him, and President Johnson sulking Achilles-like on the banks of the Pedernales because the polls no longer portrayed him as America's sweetheart.

Ambition should be made of sterner stuff.

What alarms me is the increasing reluctance of my own profession to hold still for any kind of criticism at all. The foam-flecked response of education's so-called "leaders" to Admiral Hyman Rickover's strictures a few years back could have been no more vindictively vituperative if the good admiral had stabbed their mothers.

And when Rudolph Flesch pointed out why Johnny can't read, my cap-and-gowned colleagues reacted as though Rudy had blasphemed against the Holy Ghost.

Rot.

We are not all that sacrosanct, we educators.

Pointed and pertinent criticism is, or should be, the black coffee of education. It wakes us up. If it turns out to be negative and unwarranted, it should be answered promptly, factually and in relatively civil terms, whether the comment comes from a Rudolph, a Rickover or a Rafferty.

But there is no particular need to call Flesch a mercenary incompetent, Rickover a narrow militarist or Rafferty a professional cannibal, just to make a rebuttal point.

Not that we are thin-skinned in our turn. It's just that philosophical criticism rates a philosophical defense, not wholesale billingsgate and snide questioning of the critic's motives. To respond to professional questioning with a barrage of personal invective fired from behind a screen of injured feelings is merely to confess a woeful shortage of intellectual ammunition.

The tree of education, after all, is not a sensitive plant. Or at least it shouldn't be.

THE AMERICAN TOURIST:

AN OBJECT LESSON IN INSENSITIVITY

I didn't realize what oafs we are abroad
until I became one myself . . .

> "*There is an island in the sun*
> *Where my people have toiled since time begun . . .*"
>
> CALYPSO SONG

A living, pulsing, ferny drop of emerald it is, to be sure: the isle of Martinique. Popped up like a cork from the womb of old Ocean in some forgotten cataclysm eons ago, it floats today in green and gossamer upon a sapphire sea.

Through the meshed rain forests of its rugged in-country the trade winds blow eternally among the orchid flowers of the Cassia and Flamboyant trees and hum a gentle accompaniment to the calypso music which, with its conversational lyrics and its strangely stuttering rhythm, has become the *lingua franca* of the Caribbean.

Okay. I'll knock it off before this starts sounding like one of the old Fitzpatrick travelogues, with the sun sinking slowly into the sea as we sail regretfully away. But if you've got the idea that the place grabbed me, as the kids say, you're right.

I was standing in the shadows of a 200-year-old church-
yard, watching a wedding party arrive, with the principals
emerging uncertainly from spic-and-span cars and looking around diffidently in the immemorial manner of participants in such ceremonies.

Place: Notre Dame du Sacre-Coeur de Montmartre, on
the inland outskirts of Fort-de-France, with old Mother
Pelee peeking pokerfaced between occasional rifts in the
rain clouds which are her perpetual mantilla.

Cast of characters: Four beautiful little teen-age creoles,
clad in their Sunday best, eager to be bridesmaids. An
equal number of fine-looking young ushers, in white
jackets, black ties and the Martinique equivalent of car-
nations. One bride, lustrous-eyed, with a blush like a rose
behind dark ivory. One groom, tall, straight as a royal
palm, so proud of his radiant bride that it pleased me
just to look at him.

And, of course, there was a villain. Somehow there
always is.

He was an American from my cruise ship. I recognized
him. He had an orange sweatshirt on his fat, soft belly
and a crimson beret on his fat, hard head. His striped
shorts were an affront to his sanctified surroundings, and
his greasy, smirking mustache would have raised hackles
in a saloon, to say nothing of a wedding chapel.

He emerged from the church at the precise moment
the native party was climbing the stone steps to go inside.
His little swinish eyes lit up with a beery glow, and he
brandished his camera in the very face of the startled bride.

"Hey, kid!" he bellowed condescendingly, meanwhile
blocking the way like an overweight Horatius. "Keep your

shirt on a minute while I take a shot out here in the sun. Your church is no damned good inside. Too dark."

I waited for the groom to kill him. Mentally I resigned myself to missing my boat so I could testify that the homicide was not only justifiable but positively meritorious. But nothing happened. The light had gone out of the eyes of the little wedding party. They stood on the old stone steps for a few moments, eyes downcast, a little sad, almost apologetic, while this tactful torchbearer of American culture took his rotten pictures.

Then, with a "So long, kids! Have fun!" and a familiar leer, Lord Chesterfield heaved himself out of the way and graciously permitted the wedding to proceed.

I went back to my ship and darned near got seasick all over again.

This is what's really the matter with us, I thought. Not civil rights. Not Vietnam. Not Watts. Not the Great Society.

This.

Insufferable arrogance. Contempt for anybody but ourselves. Cheerful, chuckle-headed refusal to admit that anyone is driving on the freeway except us.

I am a teacher. All my life I've fought this callous disregard for others in schools, in classrooms, in the minds and hearts of my pupils. So, also, have my million colleagues. We've failed pretty much, I guess. Never mind. We must try harder, for the stakes are high beyond belief.

Islands in the sun they are indeed. Not Martinique alone, but scores, hundreds of others, spangled and glittering across the world. Their silent, wary peoples are weighing—even as I write—our words, our deeds, our values and ourselves.

All this I thought of as I sat shaken in my stateroom. And I prayed to the God of decency and seemliness and the fitness of things to forgive me for not having clobbered that character with his own camera.

THE MEANING OF ABU SIMBEL
Lastly, something we can be proud of . . .

We are so proud of being hard-headed realists, we Americans.

Impatient with precedent, intolerant of tradition, unconcerned with convention, we think infrequently of the past and carry on a perpetual love affair with the future. This is only to be expected, I guess, of a people sprung from a stock which crossed an ocean and a continent to escape the dead hand of yesterday and to seek out a tomorrow whose promise would be limited only by the measure of the man and by the luck of the draw.

The Almighty Dollar looms larger and larger over the land, and the thoughtful European or Asiatic observer will tell you that we have built here in this hemisphere the most crassly commercial civilization in the history of the human race. We worship speed and size and science. We care little for ancient usage, and we are somewhat less than connoisseurs of art and music and the finer things of life.

I guess this is all true. Everybody says it is. But if it is true, and if everybody is right, what about Abu Simbel?

There is a blazing valley half the world away and half as old as time. There, above the confluence of the Blue Nile and the White, a treasure was laid up for us and for all men before and after us. Three thousand years and more than twice 3000 miles divide it from our modern Eden of sex, supermarkets and six-packs.

Between the First and Second Cataracts of the Nile, it towers above the mighty river in the form of the most heroic monument ever carved from living rock: the temple of Rameses. With its colossi and its cornices, its carven apes and artifacts, its halls and hieroglyphics, Abu Simbel is one of the very few really irreplaceable things on all this brawling planet.

It has no monetary value, of course. There are no fortunes to be made from its silent statues. So, when it was announced a few years back that the waters from Egypt's new Aswan Dam would cover Abu Simbel, most of us suppressed a brief sigh of regret and reconciled ourselves to the inevitability of crocodiles swimming sinuously above the sandstone corridors which once in the very dawn of history had echoed to the hammers of Pharaoh's artisans.

And lo! the worldliest decade of this, the fleshiest and most cynical of all the centuries, reared back and worked a miracle.

The nations of the world in two short years pooled their technology and sent their ablest craftsmen into the blinding heat of primeval Nubia to saw the great temple of Rameses into 30-ton blocks and then lift them bodily to higher ground for reassembly.

Abu Simbel will tower once again above Father Nile, sparkling in the rays of life-giving Ra exactly as it shone in the grand noonday of Egypt's prime, so inconceivably long ago. Mecca for the archeologist, lodestone for the historian, studio for the artist, it will stand the scrutiny of generations yet unborn, happily and paradoxically preserved by the same science which threatened to submerge it.

It has cost the world some $36 million to salvage this small but sublime segment of its past. To our lasting credit, one-third of the money was American. As the crowded centuries hurry by, it may well be the verdict of a remote posterity inhabiting a civilization impossible for us to imagine that this paltry sum was the best expenditure we ever made.

The armaments and nuclear bombs will lose their potency. The skyscrapers and the freeways will crumble into dust. The causes and disputes which overheat us so and seem of such inflated importance to us today will be dim, quaint relics of antiquity in the days beyond tomorrow.

Abu Simbel will remain.

And with it, if we are lucky, will remain a legend that the first people who possessed the skill and the techniques to work this miracle did so perform it, quietly and without undue fuss, not selfishly and for themselves alone, but for the benefit of those who will come after us on this planet. Perhaps our children's children will count it as one shining asset among the blackness of our many liabilities.

Science cannot create beauty. But it can preserve

beauty and refurbish it and hand it down the years as a rich legacy.

We who inhabit the Century of Science cannot do better than to teach our children this.

And I think it will be hard to leave behind us a better emblem of this high resolve than Abu Simbel, shimmering in the desert sun.